**CBS MarketWatch
Stories Behind the Numbers**

How America Made a Fortune and Lost Its Shirt

**CBS MarketWatch
Stories Behind the Numbers**

How America Made a Fortune and Lost Its Shirt

By Steve Gelsi

Edited by Thom Calandra

A Pearson Education Company

Copyright © 2002 by MarketWatch.com, Inc. All rights reserved. CBS and the CBS "eye device" are registered trademarks of CBS Broadcasting Inc.

All rights reserved. No part of this book shall be reproduced, stored in a retrieval system, or transmitted by any means, electronic, mechanical, photocopying, recording, or otherwise, without written permission from the publisher. No patent liability is assumed with respect to the use of the information contained herein. Although every precaution has been taken in the preparation of this book, the publisher, author, and editor assume no responsibility for errors or omissions. Neither is any liability assumed for damages resulting from the use of information contained herein. For information, address Alpha Books, 201 West 103rd Street, Indianapolis, IN 46290.

International Standard Book Number: 0-02-864261-9
Library of Congress Catalog Card Number: 2002103789

04 03 02   8 7 6 5 4 3 2 1

Interpretation of the printing code: The rightmost number of the first series of numbers is the year of the book's printing; the rightmost number of the second series of numbers is the number of the book's printing. For example, a printing code of 02-1 shows that the first printing occurred in 2002.

Printed in the United States of America

Note: This publication contains the opinions and ideas of its author and is based on information gathered in past years. It is intended to provide helpful and informative material on the subject matter covered. It is sold with the understanding that the author, editor, and publisher are not engaged in rendering professional services or advice in the book. If the reader requires personal assistance or advice, a competent professional should be consulted.

The author, editor, and publisher specifically disclaim any responsibility for any liability, loss, or risk, personal or otherwise, which is incurred as a consequence, directly or indirectly, of the use and application of any of the contents of this book.

For Marketing and Publicity, call (317) 581-3722.
The publisher offers discounts on this book when ordered in quantity for bulk purchases and special sales.
For sales within the U.S., please contact:
Corporate and Government Sales (800) 382-3419 or corpsales@pearsontechgroup.com
Outside of the U.S., please contact:
International Sales (317) 581-3793 or international@pearsontechgroup.com

Trademarks

All terms mentioned in this book that are known to be or are suspected of being trademarks or service marks have been appropriately capitalized. Alpha Books, Pearson Education, Inc., and MarketWatch.com, Inc., cannot attest to the accuracy of this information. Use of a term in this book should not be regarded as affecting the validity of any trademark or service mark.

To Jennifer and Maya

Contents

1	Losing Our Shirts	1
2	Making a Fortune	13
3	Savvy Southern Women Score	29
4	The Pros Get Shattered but Fight Back	45
5	Day Traders Hit the Brakes	59
6	African Americans Invest in Community	77
7	Stock-Picking Kids Tout the Basics	93
8	The Future at Internet Speed, for Better or Worse	107
	Index	123

Preface

Too many books on the stock market come from pundits who give a smarter-than-thou view in a professional tone. Or they're by Wall Street tycoons who offer to share some of their secrets. If they really did share their secret sauce with us, wouldn't everybody be rich?

It's time to turn the spotlight around. It's time to get inside the crowd of retail investors who have grown in power, numbers, and financial clout with the rise of the Internet. In 1999, almost 6 million households used the Internet to complete a financial transaction at an online bank/broker or seek market information at services such as CBS MarketWatch. By 2003, those 6 million households are expected to swell to 21 million, by some estimates.

This book is about you: your corner green-grocer, your retiring father-in-law, the old-timer working on the railroad, that lottery winner, your kids' school teacher, the folks in your monthly investment club.

Scanning message boards, e-mails, and media coverage, we surfed the web, traveled to the heartland to talk to investors, and mined their humor, anecdotes, and horror stories. We also touched base with the stock pros Americans love and hate.

Many who bet on high-octane shares were beaten up badly in the first bear market in 10 years, but the patterns and rules of these individual investors reveal how America handles its precious cash. There's a hunger for stocks out there. Mostly, it's because the stock market is a market of stories: 9,000 and more stories about companies, new products, ambitious executives. The stock market is America's story.

As we went to press with this book, the first to represent the stories behind the numbers at CBS MarketWatch, financial headlines were stuffed with accounting scandals at America's largest companies. The American public, ordinary folks from Bar Harbor, Maine, to Hilo, Hawaii, are being asked to understand concepts such as acquisition accounting, debt-to-equity ratios, and revenue/customer/bandwidth swaps.

In the chaos of the accounting scandals, many folks, saddled with their own retirement accounts and investing responsibilities, were frozen in the headlights. We know some older Americans who haven't made a trade in their brokerage accounts since March of 2000, when the stock market headed south. Main Street was ducking for cover. Tuning out. That's too bad. Never in modern times have ordinary investors been given such a golden opportunity to benefit from Wall Street hysteria by choosing wisely in the fiscal storm.

Anxious to recover from several years of stock market and mutual fund losses, ordinary folks are not about to be lulled back to the bull-market cradle. Smart investors have used the recent fiscal turmoil and America's military action overseas to moderate their interest in the stock market. Instead of fleeing for the exits, patient investors tend to stay invested in their favorite stocks, keep their cool despite the loud cries from nay-sayers, and even buy when the market is low, like you're supposed to do.

This book isn't a recipe for instant wealth. Rather, we give you the stories behind the numbers: why people invest in the stock market in the first place, how they go about it, and what they like to do. At the same time we also weigh in with some (but not too many) of the Wall Street pros who too often are on auto-pilot, religiously touting the stock market's virtues through good times and bad.

Now go out there and see how some of us made a fortune, others lost their shirts, and some accomplished both. As a sports-fan friend of ours tells us from his seat at the finish line, the big difference between the race track and the stock market is that, at least in the market, you get to watch them come around again.

March 2002

—Steve Gelsi, CBS MarketWatch senior reporter
—Thom Calandra, CBS MarketWatch editor-in-chief

ACKNOWLEDGMENTS

I'd like to thank CBS MarketWatch and MarketWatch.com editor-in-chief Thom Calandra, CEO Larry Kramer, and Executive Editor Dave Callaway. Compadres at CBS MarketWatch provided tireless assistance. Thanks to Julie Rannazzisi, Emily Church, Marshall Loeb, Jon Friedman, Greg Morcroft, Tomi Kilgore, Susan Lerner, Mike Baron, Allen Wan, Susan McGinnis, Alexis Christoforous, Bob Leverone, Ires Wilbanks, Roger Wallace, Ed Crane, Tom Curley, John Perugini, Mirav Ozeri, Vanessa Catalano, Chris Wall, Milena Jovanovitch, Alec Davis, Neil Chase, Jenny Spitz, Deborah Adamson, Craig Tolliver, Russ Britt, Victoria Fung, Frank Barnako, Bill Torrey, Steve Orr, Larry Kofsky, Tom Bemis, David Wilkerson, Kristen Gerencher, John Greco, Jomo Moir, Bambi Francisco, Chris Kraeuter, Erin Beach, August Cole, Tim Rostan, Chris Pummer, Rex Nutting, Jeffry Bartash, Matt Andrejczak, Irina Yuen, Pat Parker, Dima Berenboym, Scot McLernon, Suzanne Sypulski, Bill Spain, Jennifer Waters, Yuleika Saume, and others who help watch the markets all day. *The Early Show* folks, including Mark McEwen, Bryant Gumbel, Jane Clayson, Julie Chen, Lyne Pitts, and especially Stephanie Zarpas, graciously helped through their tireless work on the CBS MarketWatch Survivor™ Contest. Thanks also to Renee Wilmeth at Alpha Books for her support, Ian Donnis, who helped get me started, and my family.

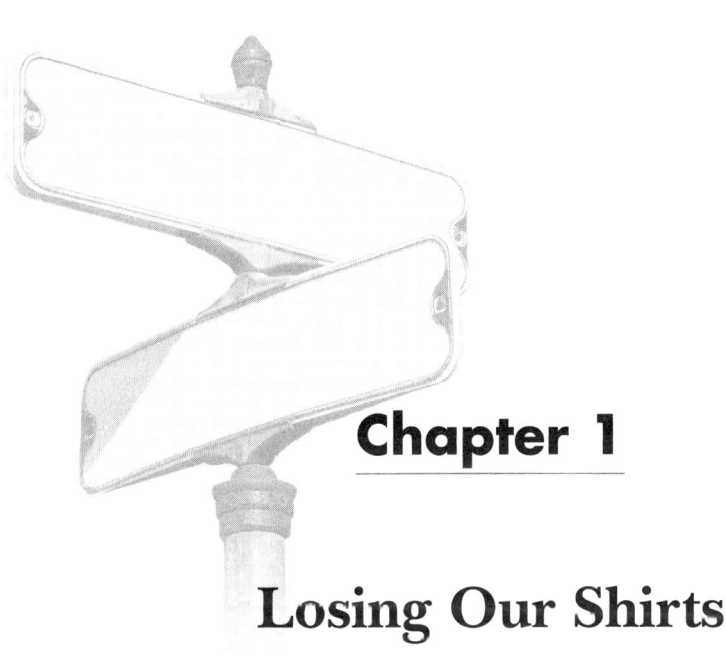

Chapter 1

Losing Our Shirts

Welcome to Main Street America's money culture, home-cooked stock picking and all.

Church members in Brooklyn, New York, pooled their community savings in the tradition of a Caribbean "su-su" as they looked to the Lord for stock market inspiration.

A Silicon Valley softball team of 20-somethings saw its best-loved technology companies go belly-up in a devastated market.

Day trader Tokyo Joe, battling government regulators, turned his nose up at traditional Wall Street brokers to become wealthy, but made some enemies along the way.

A Las Vegas schoolteacher lobbied hard for the right to teach her students what it means to make and lose money in the stock market.

An Arizona lottery winner transformed himself into a full-time investor and learned to read stock charts like a seasoned Wall Street veteran. But will he squander his fortune?

Kids at Valley Forge Middle School didn't really want to be dot-com millionaires, but they sure do love their Krispy Kreme doughnuts.

There are a million stories in the naked stock market, to tweak an adage. Ordinary folks—you and me and even your neighborhood deli owner—are out there grappling with a stock swoon that only worsened after the terrorist attacks of September 11, 2001. Some stocks fought their way back. But for most, the new century marks one of the weakest spans of stock market performance in the past hundred years. About four of every five U.S. mutual funds, the mainstay of many American investors, were stained in red ink in both 2001 and 2002. The stock market wealth that evaporated ran well into the trillions of dollars.

With war and economic woes in the news, mom-and-pop investors who saw their fortunes rise in the 1990s are finding themselves in a post-boom world. The good times may be back again sometime in the future, but one key attribute remains: Devout do-it-yourselfers continue to be a rising power on Wall Street, in either bear or bull markets. More than ever, ordinary Americans who invest in the stock market are living and dying by their own swords.

Professional money managers have a fiduciary responsibility to their clients and shareholders, but many of them are failing miserably at the business of picking stocks. The rest of us have only to answer to our spouses, our children, and the mirror at the end of each market day. Which would you rather face in the high-stakes game of personal finance?

Yet despite the downswings, stock picking is flourishing as one of the hottest national pastimes, right up there with baseball and watching DVD movies at home. The market takes us on a harrowing journey that runs our emotions ragged: elated one day, jilted the next. The players with the most money at the end of the day, week, month, and year are the winners. But not everyone comes out ahead.

For a while, the stock market seemed like a roller coaster that went up forever. It hit new highs as Wall Street cheerleaders stoked the rally with no end in sight. The more cautious investors, scoffed at during the bull market, now look a lot smarter. Their collective recipe combines basic ingredients with salt-of-the-earth common sense. Don't bet the farm. Invest a little at a time. Take baby steps before you start to run. Be wary of speculative investments. Stick to your guns even when the high-octane crowd is racing ahead.

As the twenty-first century unfolds, there's a new wariness out there. Like a movie about the Old West, investors are circling their wagons and keeping a close eye on their wallets as reports about layoffs and dwindling corporate profits fill the financial news headlines. People are looking around for their own clues, closer to home, on where the economy is headed ... and what to do with their money.

RAILROAD INDICATOR

For train conductor Jay Busby, 45, an economy in a downward spiral means the boxcars on the Burlington Northern Sante Fe railroad are transporting fewer automobiles. The Arizona resident and father of seven daughters guides his Wall Street investments by his self-dubbed index called the "Bluewater/Hibbard Railroad Indicator," based on the freight traffic rolling through the open Southwest.

"If I could bottle the information, it would be worth a million," boasted Busby, who named his prized indicator after a couple of railroad sidings along the southwestern trade route dating back to the Industrial Revolution.

The Bluewater/Hibbard Railroad Indicator sprang up unofficially in Busby's lexicon some 20 years ago as he noticed the relationship between auto shipping and the stock market. The indicator often points out downswings or upswings in the stock market up to three months ahead of time, he said. "I ride the aorta of the economy," he explained. "I feel the heartbeat of America. I do not ride a branch line. I ride the main line."

During the 1990s salad days of retail investors—when they marched by the millions into the stock market to the tune of double-digit annual portfolio gains—autos filled the freight trains out in the desert as they headed to market in the nation's metro and suburban areas. Busby noticed a decline in auto shipments shortly before the tech wreck of 2000, but the incredibly sharp move downward in the sector still caught him off guard. He was expecting an overall slowdown in the economy, not the meltdown of 39 percent in Nasdaq stocks that year.

"I can only observe the trains and their makeup," he said. "When business is good, auto racks are shipped in unit trains. When business slows, auto racks become mixed with other types of freight trains. Auto racks are the first to be taken out of storage, at least a month before the public realizes that the market has reached bottom."

The boxcar indicator doesn't work as well for picking specific stocks, but Busby claims it's guided him and others on when to buy certain shares of stocks, and the best time to dump them. "I have not kept past records of the forecast, but it does work," he said. "You don't have to be a genius to pick winners or losers when you know the direction of the economy." After September 11, 2001, Busby's Railroad Indicator pointed toward sluggishness in the economy. So he took a conservative tack.

Busby is a long-time believer in the stock market. He first bought Ramada and Occidental Petroleum stock on his own as a pipsqueak 14-year-old high school freshman. He directed his attention toward Wall Street after some frustration with the family business of raising cattle. "I had an economics teacher who had worked on the floor of the New York Stock Exchange," he recalled. "I really liked the market. I wanted to be a broker." He finally got his chance at age 30 during a break in his railroading work, but it didn't pan out as he had hoped.

Earning his license as a broker, Busby ended up selling limited partnerships in real estate deals. A popular form of investing at the time, the overall business ended up going belly-up in the face of regulatory changes and a real estate bust. "My broker let me go because I wasn't doing enough sells, and I'm glad I didn't. I didn't feel good about it."

Busby went back to the railroad, where he culled his passion for the market by developing his Railroad Indicator and advising friends on their stock picks. Needless to say, he likes railroad stocks. "The railroad is as safe as government bonds. It's gonna be there from now until the government goes broke. It's the main mover of freight. Everyone looks at the trucks, but the railroad is more efficient for hauling. One boxcar holds as much as five trucks. Railroads can always do it cheaper."

In the '90s, Busby avoided buying Internet shares "because I didn't want to invest in a company that wasn't making any money." But he embraced the Internet itself. Buying a Compaq Presario, Busby signed up for an America Online account and, like millions of other Americans, started researching the stock market over the web.

Casting his outlook for the stock market in the new millennium, Busby relies more on his own observations rather than pundits or analysts. Busby figures he may jump back into the stock market if the war against terrorism stays within bounds set in the earlier stages of the U.S. military action. "People will say it's time to get on with life. I think we'll become like the English, who have lived with (terrorism) for 30 or 40 years, and their economy still goes [on]."

Busby is eyeing shares of Palm, the maker of hand-held computers that's suffered a sharp drop in its Nasdaq-traded shares. "It's such a cheap stock—that's my buy right there," he said in late 2001. "To me, people are gonna get into these little hand-held computers. Palm sells software for everybody. Microsoft may muscle in, but if Palm gets their act together, it'll go. They've been shot down to the bottom. If you can find a tech player like Palm that's not gonna go broke, it'll go."

Busby's reluctance to invest in stocks isn't particularly unusual during bear markets. But his desire to own tech shares may go against conventional wisdom. Many investors have been burned by horrific drops in the value of technology stocks. Even after a tech stock rally that crossed into 2002, most ordinary folks are still smarting from the drop in value of the high-priced computer stocks they bought years earlier.

The way to make money on Wall Street, of course, is to move ahead of everyone else, either buying a stock that goes up, or dumping a stock before it goes down. "The belief in a thing makes it happen," famed American architect Frank Lloyd Wright once said. Well, Americans are believing at a frenetic pace these days. Average holding periods for U.S. stocks are sinking to record short spans, in some cases as little as a month, as Americans develop Internet-enabled trigger fingers with their trades. More and more Americans are venturing out on their own as entrepreneurs of sorts, managing their portfolios as startup businesses. They're self-employed fund managers for their own personal corporations, themselves—and their families.

In 2000, some 80 million Americans—about half of all U.S. households—owned stocks directly or through mutual funds, according to the most recent numbers available from the New York Stock Exchange (NYSE). That's up 86 percent from the 42 million in 1983, amid declining interest rates and a sustained bull market. Nearly everyone looked like a Wall Street genius as the Dow Jones Industrial Average, Nasdaq, and Standard & Poor's 500 (S&P 500) swelled more than 900 percent between 1980 and 1998, even before the bubble years of 1999 and 2000.

During this time, the typical stock owner changed. He or she no longer resembled the Rockefeller-like, pin-striped caricature from the Parker Brothers board game Monopoly. Rather, equity owners are now 47 years old on average, with a household income of $60,000 and up, and financial assets starting at about $85,000. They're employed and married, sharing investment decisions with their spouse. Roughly 23 million households own mutual funds exclusively. About 7 million own only individual stocks, and 18 million own a mix of mutual funds and individual stocks.

That's a bigger-than-ever universe of stock pickers, stoked by growth in employer-sponsored 401(k) plans, which introduced millions to stocks for retirement nest eggs. Among these are the more adventurous—or at least the more financially aware—folks who choose their own stocks from among the roughly 7,000 companies listed on the NYSE, Nasdaq, and American Stock Exchange.

It's fortunate that these investors are financially aware, because most of the attention is on a relatively small percentage of the stocks. Take the Dow Jones Industrial Average. The benchmark is chosen, guarded, and maintained by editors at Dow Jones, the publisher of *The Wall Street Journal*. Sure, the benchmark is made up mostly of market leaders, but it's often held out as a much wider indicator than it really is, since it's really just 30 stocks, a much thinner selection than you'd think. In fact, those 30 stocks make up just 15 percent or so of the market capitalization of the entire American stock market.

The Nasdaq index also gets a lot of attention, but a big chunk of it is derived from just seven stocks. Intel, Cisco, Microsoft, Qualcomm, Oracle, Dell, and Amgen comprise about 32 percent of the total value of the companies traded on the Nasdaq 100 based on their huge market caps. The direction of a handful of companies largely dictates the score for the 4,200 companies in the overall Nasdaq.

The Standard & Poor's 500 Index, which is owned by McGraw Hill and licensed by mutual fund giant The Vanguard Group, is a wider indicator of how the stock market is doing. The group of 500 stocks still contains only a small number of the 3,000 NYSE stocks and 4,200 Nasdaq companies in the stock-picking universe. As a group, the S&P 500 Index represents about two thirds of the market capitalization of the entire American stock market. Almost half of the stocks that trade publicly are small companies, with market values of $50 million or less. Of these, only 1 in 10 have Wall Street research written about them. There's a lot more happening in terms of stock offerings than most people realize.

So even if Joe and Josephine Sixpack, with some interest in the stock market, pay attention to the most widely quoted Wall Street reports out there, the information is still pretty much limited to the daily litany of Dow and the chosen Nasdaq few, with a small bunch of S&P blue chips thrown in for a little seasoning.

TOOL OF CHOICE

For cooking up a diverse portfolio, American investors need more. That's where the Internet comes in. Cyberspace blipped on the collective radar screen of retail investors shortly after its birth as a mass medium with the broad adoption of the Netscape web browser in the mid 1990s. More than 100 million Americans surf the web each month, according to web tracking firm MediaMetrix. The growth has been fueled by folks like Jay Busby, who have been snatching up computers as the tool of choice for tapping into Wall Street, using them to research stocks.

The most potent weapon is the online trading account, which has continued to grow even in the face of rough stock market conditions. The number of active online stock-trading accounts in the U.S. has nearly doubled from 11.6 million by the end of 1999 to 20.8 million by 2002, according to a survey of 200 brokers by research firm Gomez Associates. Alas, as stocks sold off in 2000 and 2001, the total number of assets managed online dwindled. At its peak in October 2000, 18.5 million online accounts held $1.1 trillion in assets. In the face of the bear market the following year, almost $200 billion in Internet-linked brokerage wealth dried up.

Even in the depths of the bear market of 2001, online trading continued to grab more users as a relatively affordable way to access the stock market, but the frequency of trading fell. Number-one online broker Charles Schwab, for example, said daily average trades among its roughly eight million accounts fell 34 percent in late 2001 to just under 140,000. The big hit forced thousands of layoffs at Schwab and others, as well as lower profits for brokers as they face leaner times, even as more people sign up.

As of early 2002, retail investors were not trading as much, but their passion still turned toward tech, at least among those who were surfing the web. Big names from the tech sector—Cisco Systems, Intel, Microsoft, Dell, Sun Microsystems, Oracle, AOL Time Warner, and even the sadsack on the block, Lucent Technologies—dominate the top 15 portfolio holdings at CBS MarketWatch.

The big tech companies, with stock market worth routinely north of $50 billion, are headliners in the world of mom-and-pop investors. Among the most heavily traded on Nasdaq and the NYSE, these companies grab most of the news coverage and surface in Wall Street testimonials from stock pickers around the United States. To be sure, self-styled investors have suffered some huge flameouts, among them Nortel, JDS Uniphase, and even once-bulletproof Cisco.

Decidedly absent from the list is Enron, perhaps the biggest wreck of the new decade thus far and the largest overall bankruptcy filing in U.S. history. Although the Houston-based energy trading firm rode high as a member of the S&P 500, Enron failed to grab the attention of most tech-oriented players during its heyday.

Through it all, CBS MarketWatch portfolio holders tend to adhere to a buy-and-hold philosophy, unlike many of their individual stock-trading peers. Most just don't have the time or energy to day trade in and out of stocks, so they tend to keep shares of Cisco, the imploding Lucent, and other firms caught in the tech wreck. Many ordinary folks were likely caught off guard by the market's lean years of 2000 and 2001, then decided to hold on in the hope of a gradual comeback instead of selling at the bottom.

Even fund managers continue to believe. "When the technology market stabilizes, capital-rich companies such as Cisco will be able to attract talent, make acquisitions, and introduce new products more quickly than their rivals," said optimistic fund manager Anthony Gambacorta of Preswick Capital Management in Pennsylvania. "While Cisco Systems is still expensive on a P/E basis, it merits inclusion in long-term portfolios."

You gotta believe. And most professionals and amateur dart-throwers do, at least as of writing this book in early 2002. Just don't lose sight of this: All told, some $7 trillion in stock market wealth was erased from the all-time peak of $19.1 trillion in August, 2000, to a low of $12 trillion in September

2001, according to Trim Tabs. That's one of the worst performances ever for the good old American stock market, in terms of percentage drops. With scary losses so prevalent in stocks, mom-and-pop investors parked much of their investments in money market funds and other forms of cash. Now ordinary Americans are itching to get back into the stock market with their hard-won earnings. Is this a historic quest for fulfillment? A deep-rooted desire to control destiny?

Who was it who said the greatest pitfall in a person's life is *not* to take risk? Or is the American love affair with the stock market all about greed? Flat-out, plain-as-the-raised-lettering-on-your favorite-credit-card G-R-E-E-D? Just like it was in the roaring '20s, before the crash of 1929?

Let's take a look.

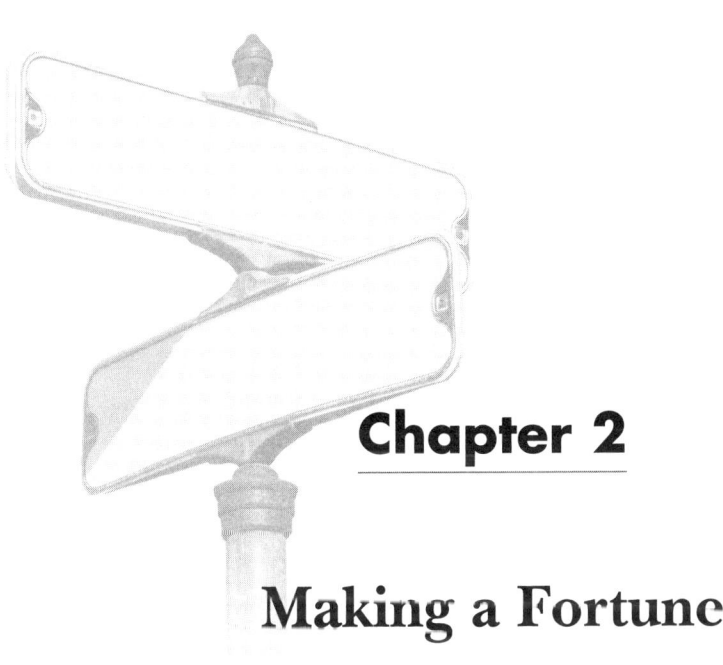

Chapter 2

Making a Fortune

With the Cold War gone by the 1990s and the governor from Arkansas in the White House, politics moved to the back burner and the attention of the nation focused on money. As the peace dividend fueled America's prosperity and interest rates fell under Fed Chief Alan Greenspan, the stage was set for the long bull market to come. Wall Street took center stage with its go-go action. This was the future. America stoked a passion for stocks, and many made a fortune.

Investment clubs, which had gained steadily over the years, accelerated in popularity as the barometer of the country's new stock-picking craze. From humble origins in Beardstown, Illinois, the Beardstown Ladies investment club helped get it all started. Initially boasting 23 percent average yearly returns that outpaced most fund managers and the S&P 500, the ladies struck a chord with everyday investors. Their fame took off like a dot-com rocket.

The club's *Common-Sense Investment Guide* sold by the hundreds of thousands with savvy advice such as how to cook up Shirley's stock market muffins, guaranteed to rise. Their favorite stock-picking ingredients included buying on the fundamentals, not on the news; weighing the company's industry ranking; and timing the right opportunity to jump into a stock. They championed the power of pooling your brain power and investing in the world around you. (Check out the parking lot at your local Wal-Mart, and if it's crowded every time you go, think about buying their stock.)

The Beardstown Ladies had a great and memorable ride through the TV talk show circuit as their books and other brand extensions flew off store shelves. But the Ladies' fame hit the skids when an independent audit revealed portfolio gains closer to the high single-digit range. Not bad, but nothing to brag about. Apparently muffins weren't the only things they were cooking. Some have quipped they might have been cooking the books, too, either intentionally or by mistake.

Despite their downfall, the Ladies' do-it-yourself message inspired countless amateur chefs to start brewing up their own gains on Wall Street. In the early 1990s, about 8,300 investment clubs belonged to the National Association of Investors Corporation, the Royal Oak, Michigan, umbrella group for investment clubs and publisher of *Better Investing* magazine. By 1998, the number of clubs peaked at an incredible 37,000 as the bull market reached its height.

With a median age of 53 and household income topping $100,000, the ranks of the roughly 400,000 individuals enrolled in clubs registered with the NAIC prefer to stock up on the nation's biggest companies. Collectively, their favorite stock picks include Intel, Home Depot, Cisco Systems, and Merck. They hold stocks an average of four years. The personal portfolio of the average member is worth $301,300.

The average club asset total is $63,100. Most of the clubs are organized as general partnerships with federal Employer Identification Numbers required to open up a brokerage account. Members usually pick stocks based on a majority vote; others weigh votes by total ownership percentage.

Once a bastion of men, the groups have evolved to contain 54 percent all-female groups. Overall, 69 percent of all investment club members of women. It turns out that women are better at stock picking anyway. During 1999, the average compounded annual lifetime earnings rate for all-female clubs was 32 percent, nearly 10 points ahead of the average 23 percent return for all-guy groups. Co-ed clubs earned an average return of 27.4 percent.

Overall, the NAIC preaches a safer path on Wall Street. Another group out there with a conservative bent is the American Association of Individual Investors. Collectively, they believe in the tortoise, not the hare. In a bear market, they look good. In a bull market, they look stodgy. But investors at these home-grown clubs say that if you stick to their rules, you can make money.

PLENTY OF SENSE

Food and finance go arm-in-arm in Chicago, home of the Mercantile Exchange, where commodities, stock futures, and options are heavily traded, as well as the most mouth-watering steaks in the heartland. Back in September of 1992, eight Chicagoans who knew decidedly more about food than finance decided to start nibbling on stocks as well—not soup stock, company stock. One couple and a few culinary chums already enjoyed meeting regularly for Louisiana Cajun food or grilled steak washed down with homemade Sangria. Many had known each other since high school; a few traced their friendships back to grammar school. Two of the women initiated talk about forming an investment club, and finally all eight people agreed, explained one member, a scholarly figure with a beard and white hair.

Faced with their initial naiveté about the stock market, the Chicagoans decided their investing strategy made no sense. As time went on, they rallied around the objective of making only big dollars instead of pennies. Ergo, they dubbed themselves the No Cents Investment Club.

For No Cents, a focus on food continued. The group kept the tradition of meals as they gathered around their kitchen and dining room tables to feast on one Saturday each month. Between bites, the group honed the fundamentals of stock picking with gurus such as Peter Lynch, the Fidelity Investments honcho with big, white hair of TV commercial fame. They also liked Warren Buffett, a perennial favorite among investment clubs. Buffett, the Omaha, Nebraska-based chief of holding company Berkshire Hathaway, also loves edible stocks such as McDonald's and Coca-Cola.

"Between Warren Buffett and us, we own 200 million shares of Coke," the group joked. No Cents decided early on to take a more cautious approach to the market. "We do not day trade or follow any fad," is their boiled-down motto.

Armed with aprons and wooden spoons, No Cents said it cooked up an equally tasty portfolio. The overall stock-picking strategy was very meat and potatoes—traditional, filling, and rarely dangerous.

"We like long-term, steady companies showing steady growth, and top in their sector," they said. Besides Coca-Cola, they've picked Walgreen, Applied Materials, Cisco, ETrade, Halliburton, Motorola, and SPX, among others. One member said their favorite is probably Walgreen, since it's based in their area and offers steady growth and dividends. Among their flameouts was Callaway Golf, whose stock went up after they bought it, only to get lost in the rough.

Majority rule determined which stocks were bought or sold. When buying, the group tried to compare at least three companies within an industry before making a decision. With such cautious wisdom under its collective belt, it wasn't long before No Cents started seeing the dollars grow. The group claimed an average annual return of 11 percent per year or greater in the 1990s—not great in the boom years, but pretty good in terms of outperforming inflation and coming out ahead with their money. By the end of the decade, each of the four couples had invested about $11,000 each, while throwing in monthly dues of $50. They had fun doing it, too, not to mention some good meals.

Not only could they pick stocks, the No Cents members were ready for the spotlight. In a team video* submitted to CBS MarketWatch, they put themselves on the covers of mocked-up versions of financial magazines. One woman appeared on the cover of so-called *Young Investor* with a big smile and long brown hair. Another chose the cover of *Market Watcher* magazine. Another woman posed for the front of *Wall Street Woman*, while her husband headlined *Wealth Builder* magazine. The latter title is apparently the only one from an actual magazine. The others were made up for fun.

The video portrayed their stock picking techniques: intimidation, using the Magic Eight Ball toy, and trying to read butterfly ballots left over from the 2000 election. "This isn't going to work, my chad didn't come through," one joked, referring to the notorious problems with poorly punched voting cards in Florida that had to be counted by hand during the 2000 presidential contest.

No Cents was wise to chase the spotlight, since investment clubs and individual investors often end up generating attention. Money talks in America, and Wall Street gurus and anyone else who touts how to make millions are a staple on TV shows. Anyone with a good money tale to tell is a hot media commodity, especially mom-and-pop investors who cook up their own portfolios. The Beardstown Ladies were proof of that.

While No Cents isn't big on dividend-paying stocks, they do keep an eye on them. The equities are often on the radar screen of other conservative investors. Like interest from a bank account or any other income, owners have to pay taxes on earned dividends, but it's a solid way to cook up some investment gains in an uncertain environment. A survey of top dividend-paying companies and their trading symbols by Morningstar in late 2001 includes the following:

ENI S.p.A. (stock trading symbol, E)
American Israeli Paper Mills (AIP)
BNS Company (BNS)
REIT Philips International Realty (PHR)
Capstead Mortgage (CMO)
Great Northern Iron Ore (GNI)
Alstom SA (ALS)
Smith & Nephew (SNN)
Washington Post (WPO)
1st State Bancorp (FSBC)

Getting fancy with the numbers, Morningstar, a stock market research company, also divides yearly dividends per share by profits per share to come up with a list of the companies with the biggest payout ratios also in late 2001:

Trenwick Group (TWK)
Elsevier NV (ENL)
Russell Corp. (RML)
Dow Chemical (DOW)
West Pharmaceutical Services (WST)
Olin (OLN)
Dillard's (DDS)
Clarion Commercial Holdings (CLR)
PLM International (PLM)
Blimpie International (BLM)
Tanger Factory Outlet (SKT)

The most interesting thing about the two lists of the dividend leaders is that they get little or no hype. That makes them worth a closer look by any collection of contrarian do-it-yourself stock pickers.

Another popular option in rough stock times is equities that reflect the value of gold. Such stocks were shunned during the high-flying 1990s, but always come back into vogue every now and then. Some of the more widely held gold stocks in early 2002 include:

Newmont Mining (NEM)
Barrick Gold Corp. (ABX)
Anglogold (AU)
Placer Dome (PDG)
Gold Fields (GOLD)

BOOMTOWN SAN FRANCISCO AND TEAM FOUCHEK

Most didn't play it safe during the happy days of the 1990s. There were plenty of risk takers, as the somber-minded voices were drowned out in all the Internet-flavored hype. Betting on tech and even riskier Internet upstart companies out of New York, Silicon Valley, and elsewhere paid off big for a while.

Much of it came out of San Francisco, the place where high tech is grown in the form of budding startups, at least during the 1990s. The town that boomed in the California Gold Rush shifted into high gear once again as young technology entrepreneurs went on mad hiring and office-building sprees with cash from even younger venture capitalists.

Starbucks-guzzling 20-somethings put on their chinos, t-shirts, and fleece vests and poured into the city, filling their schedules with cocktail parties, apartment parties, sports, outdoor adventures, dating, and lots and lots of work, work, work. One of the big incentives: stock options if your company went public.

Powering the digital merry-go-round was a huge stream of initial public offerings (IPOs) that investors gobbled up like chocolate-covered raisins. And it was quite easy to go public for a time. IPO investors devoured shares of Internet retailers—glorified catalog merchants. But they soon tired of them after a flood of deals from investment bankers that pocketed millions in the deals.

The spotlight moved to Internet business companies focused on using the web to streamline accounting and procurement. That lasted a few months. Then the magic phrase became "Internet infrastructure." The idea: Get rich by investing in the companies that made the pickaxes and Levis jeans in the new economy gold rush. In 1999 and 2000, nearly 1,000 companies went public in the United States as retail investors and other speculators pushed the market to its peak. (In contrast, fewer than 100 companies went public in the bear year of 2001.) IPOs turned employees into retail stock investors. You would normally have to open up your own trading account to cash in your shares, and from there you would be in the market.

For a new generation of Wall Street investors, the boom was all they knew, so they believed in it. To many, the so-called Generation X owned the new economy. They worked at the dot-coms and they bet on Internet stocks. One icon of the 20-somethings was Stuart, the quirky red-haired pitchman for online broker Ameritrade. He became briefly famous in TV ads that showed him introducing his 50-something boss to Internet stock buying and doing a crazy dance when the older guy executed his first trade. "Let's light this candle!" Stuart would say.

Kevin Vasquez of San Francisco was working for Commerce One in Silicon Valley as a young sales associate when the Internet software firm went public in early 1999 at $21 per share. Like most dot-com employees, Kevin got options that would guarantee him a profit if the stock rose. And rise it did, as the Nasdaq took off. By the end of 1999, Commerce One shares had shot up past $50. The company filed a lightning-fast, 2-for-1 stock split. By early 2000, during the height of the bubble, the stock rose to $100 per share. All was good.

During the rush, Vasquez and a few of his softball team buddies decided to form an investment club. Flush with their newfound status at the helm of the biggest tech boom in recent history, the guys cast around for a name. They came up with Fouchek. Details of its precise origins are sketchy, beyond the explanation that it comes from the moniker of a friend from Lake Tahoe in California. They also used the Fouchek name for their softball team. But there is no guy named Fouchek in the club. The name is just one of those many random things floating out there in the universe.

Team Fouchek members have high-risk, high-reward jobs, so they aimed to set up a high-risk, high-reward investment club. They mixed in lots of testosterone, and took their best shot. Soon, their ranks swelled to include 14 guys in their late 20s and early 30s. They bet on marquee tech firms close to home: Oracle, Intel, Cisco, and Sun Microsystems, as well as high-flying Internet stocks such as Internet Capital Group.

Apparently, betting on the stock market wasn't risky enough for Fouchek. They wanted to go to Las Vegas, too. Their primary investment goal was to raise $1.4 million, or $100,000 per member, for a trip to the gambling mecca. The soon-to-come tech wreck of 2000–2001 deflated this dream, but they still make a trip to Vegas every now and then on their wages. They hold their meetings in cyberspace, preferring e-mail to regular meetings. They get together at least once every quarter to talk stocks over pizza and beer. A stylized video profile made by the team resembles an episode of MTV's show *Real World* and provides a glimpse into their stock-picking world.

A jazzy flute plays as a superimposed image appears of a devil caricature with wads of cash grasped in its hands. The camera scrolls down a list of signatures from the Fouchek Investment Club members before cutting to an apartment party. Voices of dot-com revelers flare up. Each guy takes his turn standing next to the refrigerator and talking to the camera. At the bottom of the screen flashes a mini resumé in lowercase white letters listing name, employer, and title in the Fouchek Investment Club. Ranjit Bhonsle appears along with several others to lend their voices to the effort.

They keep their remarks short in a rapid-fire tempo. "We are a group of guys interested in the financial market. We talk about it all the time, so why not do something about it?" says Kevin Vasquez, who has long, wavy hair and wears a fleece vest with a long-sleeved white t-shirt. Another founding member of Fouchek in a sweater with a white t-shirt begins to speak, but is interrupted. "Look at those shoes, they look like a platypus!" someone says. The camera pans down to his trendy, flat-toed dress shoes as he wags his foot.

"With patience and persistence, I think we're going to be profitable," another Fouchek fellow says confidently. "We also have an edge to us. We have attitude with Silicon Valley brain power." One guy in a floppy hat and gray t-shirt holds a frothy beer against his chest. He boasts, "I hold my current company's record for consecutive days wearing shorts to work." "No way, you have not worn pants?" someone asks.

The narrator says, "There's tons of buffoonery in this room. There's tons of characters. And it just goes beyond simple investing. It's a big group of friends that just laugh at each other and invest on the side." Another guy concludes, "Every member of this club is an aspiring capitalist."

Brian Townsend of BMC Software, another founding member, appears as a figure in the shadows. The little that can be seen through the dark reveals the face of a clean-cut guy with a slightly crazed look in his eye. "If I don't invest well, and if I don't make money in this investment club … I will drive off the Golden Gate Bridge." You don't believe him when he says that, but you know he may be thinking about it, because he's deep …. At the end of the video, all of the Fouchek members applaud.

THE REST OF THE COUNTRY JUMPS ONBOARD

But the happy days didn't just happen in California to guys (and gals) in their 20s. The ranks of stock market newbies were filled en masse by older Americans who gathered to build up their nest eggs. In retirement havens such as Florida, investing on Wall Street has thrived more than bingo and shuffleboard. The heady days of stock market gains also incited wacky behavior in New England, the Rocky Mountains of Colorado, and the plains of the Midwest.

The Polaris Investment Club of Riviera Beach, Florida, formed in 1994 in the hope of moving their finances northward. With silver hair and a voice that sounded like a narrator from a World War II documentary, its founding member said the group of men and women was inspired by the North Star, Polaris. "For centuries, it was the principal means of ancient navigators showing them the way to navigate, often through troubled waters," he said. "I liken investing to that. With knowledge, one has the power of direction and control."

As Polaris became a fixture in the stock market culture of Florida, they fashioned their own set of matching turquoise team polo shirts, embroidered with a gold shooting star, red beams of light, and the name of their club in white. The group of 14 people—a schoolteacher, two accountants, a physician, four retirees, two business owners, an administrator, and others—met in the clubhouse of a country club in Palm Beach Gardens. Munching on pretzels and Pop Tarts, members teed off with their favorite stock picks. They first chose to buy Merck, the blue chip pharmaceutical company that does a lot of business down in the Sunshine State. A retiree and self-described Internet addict, the founder summed up the group's style as "no nonsense," with bets on Stryker, Home Depot, and Aflac. They nibbled on tech with an investment in Applied Materials, a maker of equipment used to manufacture silicon chips. The group took first place in 1997 and 1999 in the Annual Portfolio Contest by the South Florida Council of the National Association of Investors Corporation.

"We take investing quite seriously and realize we are building something that hopefully our children and grandchildren will someday assume," the founder said. Polaris has built up a serious war chest, too. By the start of 2001, they had invested $186,000 and built up a portfolio worth about $360,000.

Meanwhile, up in New England in the late 1990s, a group of women at their jobs at a Silicon Highway tech company off of Massachusetts Route 128 walked into a meeting room on their lunch break. They took off their white lab coats, rolled up their sleeves, and started stock picking. This was the routine of the Forest Street Investors, who designed a team banner decorated with evergreen trees and money symbols. One member read *The Wall Street Journal* and reported to the group on moves in the economy. In a team video, she dresses up like Rich Uncle Pennybags, the bushy-moustached character that appears in the game Monopoly.

"In a normal work day, we're scientists and engineers," says the narrator. "But at lunch time on meeting days, we become the Forest Street Investors." Someone in the room rings a bell and they start trading. "We should buy Cisco," one woman says. "We should sell Home Depot, it's been a dog lately," says another.

They display some vaudevillian schtick by hanging stock chits to dry on a clothesline and coyly asking, "Are you sure this is what they mean by online trading?" Afterwards, they stand around and give each other high fives as the Pink Floyd song "Money" plays.

Club members said Forest Street has made money and stoked friendships, despite the ups and downs of the market. Even after co-members resigned from the company where they all worked, they still remained in the group. One woman left to become a schoolteacher. She stands in front of a poster that says "Einstein Asked Questions" and says her biggest investment isn't in stocks, but in helping kids enrich their future. Another member who moved on to become a therapist says, "I'm the one who went back to graduate school for psychology and I'm really glad I did in this crazy market so I can help to keep us all just a little calmer."

Circle City Investment Club of Indianapolis tied its club culture to the fast race cars that give the city its fame. "We live in the racing capital of the world," said Tony May, a bespectacled midwesterner. "We've tried to maintain a focus on racing in our investing policies and practices." The club, which started rolling in August 1997, is made up of professionals from some of the employers in the area, including Rolls Royce and Thomson Electronics, but they haven't lost their playful perspective.

They wove their responsible lives as serious stock investors with their passion for cars. Each year, the group helped raise money for charity by holding an annual stock car race with model cars. In a team video, they settle stock-picking disputes by casting their lot with a race car. One guy bets on a car for bank MBNA, the other bets on a car for Home Depot. The fastest car down a makeshift ramp is added to the team's portfolio.

The Hogback Investment Club of Golden, Colorado, ties its local inspiration to the area's history as a center for precious metal prospecting, more than its other noteworthy roots as a haven for Harley-Davidson riders and the birthplace of brewing monolith Coors. Their name comes from a local mountain range called Hogback, where miners dug for gold, the equivalent of hot stocks more than 100 years ago. "Our group pans for stock the way our ancestors panned for gold," members chime in a team video. They meet in a large, chalet-type living room with a stone fireplace, chimney, and vaulted ceilings. The group is made up of 11 women, age roughly 40 to 50. In the video they scurry around the room, which is decorated with little piggy banks. Joyce Jennings wears a pig outfit with ears and a nose. "Sometimes we goof and we mistake fool's gold for the real thing," they say.

Their stock picks include Cisco, General Electric, and Pfizer. They bought Wendy's because they enjoy snacking on food from the restaurant chain. They lost big on an IPO from Cavion in late 1999. "We've won some and we've lost some, but our stocks have indeed panned out. ... We're willing to take a risk, we're all women, we're tenacious as hogs, and we're all students of investing."

The happy days of the 1990s were simple and joyous for stock picking. And most investors hope those days will return sooner rather than later. Stock picking has flourished because it connected with Americans and their major passions: competition and money. The other thing Americans love most is winning, and in the '90s, nearly everyone could boast some kind of gain. Initial public offerings thrived, grabbed the spotlight, and stoked even more interest.

From Chicago to San Francisco, from Indianapolis to Riviera Beach, Florida, and everywhere in between, you could find them—folks gone wacky over the stock market as they followed their own paths to hopeful prosperity. The stock market, with all its ups and downs, daily heartbreaks, and genuine bull-market scores, had become a spectator sport. So who needs the Super Bowl, anyway?

*The team video by No Cents and other videos cited in this chapter came from applications for the CBS MarketWatch Survivor™ Contest, a stock-picking competition. Granted, the groups hammed it up to get picked, but the videos provide a true glimpse into the bullishness of the era.

Chapter 3

Savvy Southern Women Score

The stock market gets trillions of dollars from people who work in places like Spartanburg, South Carolina. Although many may not realize it, Spartanburg's location in the Southeast places it within the largest percentage of equity owners in the U.S. Some 33 percent of the country's stockholders live in the South, compared to 26 percent in the Midwest, 25 percent in the West, and 16 percent in the Northeast, according to the Investment Company Institute.

One popular recipe for success around the region is to be wary of brokers. Use them wisely, but not without your own research. And don't just rely on a piggy bank to grow your money, when on average, stocks provide greater returns. A glimpse at the inner workings of stock investing Spartanburg-style reveals an emphasis on brains, research, hunches, and a bit of gossip about local dealings. Mix it all with a little debutante flair, and you have the Piggy Bank Investments Club.

Stretching back in time to trace the origins of the city's money trail, the burg first became a distinct commerce-generating entity during the Revolutionary War. The Greek name of Sparta, taken from an ancient city known for its austere and athletic residents, was attached to the region in a letter dated September 11, 1775, from resident Colonel John Thomas to William Drayton, a patriot and landowner. Drayton supplied some of the pro-independence locals—the so-called Spartan regiment—with supplies and ammunition, and was warmly received on a visit with a meal of barbecued beef, as noted by local historians. Even in early times, the good people of Spartanburg loved their barbecue.

It's never been determined if the Spartan regiment of the Revolutionary War was named for the town, or if the town was named for the regiment. Back then, no one really cared. The important thing was to fight the British and set up an independent nation that would eventually build the New York Stock Exchange. The town's ties to the Revolutionary War continue to this day with a statue of General Daniel Morgan, a hero of the Battle of Cowpens. He stares mightily over the citizens in a downtown square.

At the turn of the twentieth century, Spartanburg's position as a railroad center earned it the nickname Hub City. Some in town still talk about this period as the town's golden age, when artists and wealthy folks like the Vanderbilts were drawn there from all over the country. After World War II, the city's downtown lost out to automobile-inspired strip malls nearby, like many municipalities. It's managed to fight back somewhat, but it still trails the more gentrified core of nearby rival Greenville.

Nowadays, mom-and-pop stock market players from Spartanburg get their 401(k) money to invest from their jobs at the region's big employers: schools, universities, hospitals, and government offices. German auto maker BMW, which made national headlines in the '90s with its decision to build a major car plant in the region, is still thriving. Many auto-related businesses, including French tire maker Michelin, have a significant presence. The textile industry, a big employer since the late nineteenth century, has been in decline for years. The economic slowdown in the U.S. has generated thousands of layoffs in the region. But overall, employment remains relatively strong.

Noted wealthy residents of Spartanburg include the Milliken family, an industrial dynasty that traces its roots to the wool business in Maine after the Civil War. Milliken & Company is now one of the world's largest privately held companies. Roger Milliken still lives in town in a stately home surrounded by tall rows of neatly trimmed hedges.

Jerry Richardson, owner of the NFL football team the Carolina Panthers, was a football star at Wofford College in Spartanburg before he started Spartan Food Systems. The company later became a part of Advantica, the parent of Denny's restaurants, housed in the tallest building in Spartanburg, a 19-story concrete monolith that towers over the two-story shops in the center of town. Along the way, Richardson left the company to establish the Panthers at Ericsson Stadium, about an hour away in Charlotte, North Carolina.

George Dean Johnson was the country's largest franchiser of Blockbuster Video stores, which he sold in 1993 to Viacom. Now he's CEO of Extended Stay America, which is establishing a new headquarters building in the middle of town. He's also chairman of Advance America, a check-cashing specialist. His name often comes up in local conversations.

These are the local bigwigs who can afford to hire the best money managers to handle their stock picks on Wall Street. Not so with Susan Jackson, a writing professor at Spartanburg Technical College, who had no millions to play with. She was just trying to get the best return for whatever she could stash away in her 401(k) or savings. Relying in the past on brokers, she decided to take more control over her portfolio, like her grandmother on her mother's side taught her as a girl.

Jackson's grandmother, Mary Belle Crosland, raised two daughters mostly on her own in Winsboro, South Carolina, built rental houses, and launched a florist business by growing flowers in her back yard and selling them in her sun room. Trained as a teacher but not fond of the profession, she ended up buying a greenhouse to grow her stock. She also planted a seed of commerce in her granddaughter's head.

"She didn't have a cash register, you never saw where money changed hands," Jackson recalled as a girl watching her grandmother sell flowers. "I realized all her money went into a gold cigar box in a buffet in the dining room." Her grandmother would ask her to count the money, usually several hundred dollars. "She would say we'll take it and just spend the interest off the top. She was a hard-working woman, and she knew the value of money. Looking in the gold cigar box showed me the security that money brings ... not happiness, but security."

Taking her hard-earned flower earnings, Crosland invested in shares of Esso, the predecessor of Exxon, partly because a cousin owned an Esso gas station. When she died in 1980, she owned about a half-dozen stocks and an estate worth about $125,000, built up from nothing.

The lessons stayed with Susan Jackson after she got married, had kids, and started thinking about the stock market again in the 1990s. Jackson's father, Henry Beckham, had handed some of his retirement money over to a broker, but he lost a five-figure sum in junk bonds. "After that, he decided that from now on, all the mistakes will be his own fault, not some broker's fault," Jackson said. Along the way, he joined the Andrew Jackson Investment Club, to help him watch his money. He urged his daughter to do the same.

Remembering granny, and armed with the bylaws from her father's club, Jackson hooked up with her friend Mary Olejnik, who possesses a side-splitting comedic ability mixed with a distinct Southern drawl. Turning up her accent for emphasis, Olejnik said the group formed and quickly picked a name to set a tongue-in-cheek tone. "We were thinking of two names, Piggy Bank and Ladies of the Evening, but we decided that Piggy Bank was a little more becoming. The name doesn't necessarily give us much more respect, but it's pretty accurate." It was 1993.

They may be deft at their manners, charms, and self-effacing remarks, but these women are no cupcakes. Underneath a whopping sense of humor, they possess a steely toughness and some first-class brains. One is a family court judge, another a paralegal in a powerful local real estate law firm. Others are business people or teachers. All are survivors with families, jobs, social lives, and plenty of world experience. Although they criticized themselves for their decision to sell Pfizer right before the stock skyrocketed upon news of its potency drug Viagra, at least they were smart enough to buy the stock in the first place and make money on it.

In our talks, the group exudes passion for food, friends, family, gossip, money, and the South. Susan Jackson and fellow Piggy Bank member Bobbi Duncan (who in late 2001 started up a volunteer tutoring program for senior citizens to teach kids) proudly point out that their daughters recently completed their debuts. Although they consider themselves modern working women, Duncan and Jackson couldn't resist the seduction of the Magnolia Debutante Club, one of the city's exclusive social clubs complete with curtseys, formal waltzes, and white gloves. Mothers and daughters bond over lessons in manners, etiquette dinners, and a season of parties. Duncan, an Ohio native, said that at first, her Southern lawyer husband objected to her taking part in the Debutante Club, but after her daughter's friends got involved, there was no more fighting it. Jackson proudly carries a stunning picture of her daughter Kassie, resplendent with long blond hair, satin gown, and an appearance that more closely resembles Marcia Brady in a prom episode of *The Brady Bunch* than, say, Scarlett O'Hara.

Mixing their Southern savvy and collective ability to suss out stocks, the Piggy Bank Investments Club boasted an annual rate of return of 10 percent by early 2001. Each of the 14 members had invested $2,400 for a total kitty of almost $34,000. General Electric and Johnson & Johnson topped their list of favorites. Their main villain stock was Fonar, which just kept going down. "Piggy Bank investors means we use our spare change to invest with and not to take ourselves too seriously," Duncan explained, referring to the group's mantra of buying an imaginary oceanfront house and plenty of plastic surgery. "We are inspired by that beach in the sky and all those face-lifts!"

Cool air descended on a quiet, tree-lined Converse Heights neighborhood of large homes on the old-moneyed Eastern side of town. But during a monthly meeting on September 10, 2001, no less, inside the home of Georgia Anderson, the Piggy Bank Investments Club was starting to heat up.

In the large living room, a handsome collection of 10 Southern women, aged 40 and up, sipped blush wine and nibbled on little triangle-shaped sandwiches with the crusts cut away. Smiling piggy banks of various colors decorated the dining room and coffee tables. The finger food provided a light but delicious base for honed stock picking.

Most of the members of the club were present at the meeting. They wrote out $90 checks for their dues to the club. Conversation touched on Mary Olejnik, president and co-founder of the club, who was absent because she was throwing a party for her son's Eagle Scout promotion that night. Someone mentioned the bleak stock market and whether it would turn around in 2002. Most didn't think so. Folks settled into their seats and broke the ice with a joke. "You know the difference between a Northern and Southern fairy tale?" one woman asked. "The Northerner says, 'Once upon a time …' and the Southerner says, 'Y'all aren't gonna believe this!' That's a clean North/South joke."

The pun set a light tone for the night as women debated stocks and gossiped at the same time. Sometimes the gossip actually helped them pick stocks, at least when they considered local companies that employ people they know.

But this night, a more somber topic faced them. They have seen some of the worst losses since founding the club some eight years ago. Even on the eve of the September 11, 2001, terrorist attacks, when these women were meeting, the group had seen rough results. The 14 members collectively owned 14 stocks. All but one were down sharply. In one month, their combined worth had dropped from $33,492.73 to $28,955.46. As the lead character in the animated film *Shrek* would say, "This is the part where *you* run away."

AmSouth Bank fell from $19.77 per share to $18.25; AT&T went from $20.34 to $17.70; Cisco fell from $19.63 to $14.36; and even mighty Citigroup dropped mightily from $50.26 to $43.42. Disney fell from $26.88 to $24.11, and the Gap fell from $27.16 to $14.99. Harley-Davidson went from $52.09 to $43.93, and Intel dropped from $30.22 to $25.89.

Oracle was nearly halved from $17.57 to $11.07, and solid little Regions Financial was down to $28.30 from $32.31. Safeway deflated from $45.32 to $43.67, and Skechers waned from $21.85 to $19.50. Life continued to sputter out for the dog of the group, Fonar, down from $1.87 to a measly $1.71. Johnson & Johnson hung in there, actually edging *up* from $55.33 to $55.73.

"This was one of our worst months ever," said Susan Jackson, who conducted the meeting in the absence of Olejnik. The name of the Beardstown Ladies then came up in the context of investment clubs and their stock gains. "I wonder how they're doing now?" asked one member. "It turns out that they weren't doing nearly as well as they thought," Jackson said. "They were cookin' the books," joked Dottie Weaver, a retired retailer, widow, and member of the Calvary Baptist Church. "One thing's for sure, we aren't cookin' the books here," Jackson added. "We're just gonna go down as the group that has a fine time together."

The round-table style continued through the night, as women peppered the evening with jokes, finished each other's sentences, and free-associated about their stocks and how their portfolio was doing. "We have done fine (in the past)," said Jackson. "Not great, but not badly up until recently. Now, we're in the worst financial shape that we've ever been in. Our bottom line is very bad. I hate to say it, but it's bad. The only stock that we made any money on was Johnson & Johnson. The Gap lost 50 percent in one month. Oracle lost 50 percent this month." The room grew quiet. "Oh, shhhhh ... Chicago," one woman said, instead of saying "SH*T!" Jackson continued, "Skechers didn't do much better ... I just think retail is not the thing to do right now. I'm sorry and that's that."

There was some good news, however. The group made a healthy chunk of cash by selling its shares of General

Electric, a long-time component of their portfolio. They unloaded it at $41 per share and made about $9,500. "We made good money on GE," Jackson said. "We made a lot of money on GE, so we decided to go ahead and sell it, before it bottomed out."

Despite the apparently dire state of their portfolio, the women seemed surprisingly calm. Most had already been tracking the club's stocks on their own, so they already knew the news was bad. But still, Jackson's dire description of their portfolio failed to produce a ripple of panic or fever to sell. The group was also buoyed by its sale of General Electric, which left them with $12,000 including cash on hand. Although it was a buying month for the women, they seemed reluctant to jump in given the bear market conditions.

They calmly proceeded with the meeting by updating each other on stocks in their portfolio and whether to buy, sell, or hold. Most said they wanted to hang on to stocks, despite drops in stock prices that would send many other investors out the door. "AmSouth is down from 18 to 13, but it's still a hold," said Margaret Allen, an interior designer. "But we're still makin' money on that (from when we bought it)."

Karen Harpe, a teacher, was up next with Ma Bell. "AOL Time Warner is said to be pursuing AT&T's cable unit. That would make AOL the largest cable Internet provider if they buy out AT&T. So that's a possible ... merger. So that would be good for us."

Cathy Ayers, a pharmacist, was up next. "Citigroup is down this month, but I feel it is still a hold," she said. "It's holding its own in a bad market. I think it's still a good stock. And my mother is acquiring shares of Citigroup."

"Is she really?" asked one member. "That gives us hope ..."

"Usually her ideas are better than the brokers'," Ayers pointed out. "I generally think she has done better. She did well with Wachovia. She has dumped every bit of Wachovia. She thinks it's time to get out of Wachovia."

"Listen to your mom," another member whispered.

Disney was next. Martha McDaniel, nutrition program coordinator and clothing retailer, launched into her update. "What I've read and what they're saying is that they were doing all that downsizing," she said. "Their earnings are not, in the next few quarters, going to reflect what people want them to, but the company is really pleased with what they're seeing going on. ... They expect in 2002 to see their earnings increase, which is good news in the long run."

Georgia Anderson jumped in with her update on the Gap. "It's been a bad month for retailers ... they lost ... oooh ... 50 percent (of their stock value)," she said. "I think they're predicting they're gonna lose some more next quarter, but ..."

"They have some bad designs in there," someone said. "My kids didn't even buy. I've been in there and nothing appealed to me."

"They've done a lot of restructuring," Georgia said. "And I think they're down so much, we ought to hold it and see if it goes back up. But as soon as it gets back to where we're close to getting our money back ...."

"For the Gap to be down when it's back-to-school time, I think that's just a bad sign," said one.

"All the retailers are down."

"The unemployment rate is way up now ...."

"When the economy's down ... people are holding on to their money."

"We mommas aren't gonna give our teenagers any money."

Despite the poor performance of the Gap, no one suggested selling it at that moment.

Dottie Weaver proceeded with Harley-Davidson, a stock that she follows in part through her son, who owns a coveted dealership for the red-hot company. "They announced today that the board of directors approved a quarterly cash dividend," Weaver read with a hint of triumph in her voice.

"Yay!"

"How many shares do we have?"

"Forty-two."

"So we'll be able to buy a bush for our [imaginary] beach house," one woman said. No one even mentioned the idea of selling Harley-Davidson, a steady performer with legendary brand strength and a devoted customer base.

Next up: presenting possible purchases. Robin, Bobbi, Margaret, and Susan had stocks to pitch for the club to buy.

Susan Jackson mentioned Extended Stay, a lodging firm founded by local Spartanburg business magnate George Dean Johnson and Wayne Huizenga, chairman of Auto Nation. The Piggy Bank Investments Club owned the stock after it kicked up a lot of local attention when the company was formed in the mid 1990s. They sold the shares in 1997.

A small article that ran in the local paper, but was not widely reported nationally, caught Jackson's eye. She clipped it out and brought it to the meeting. "This article was in the paper last Friday. 'Bill Gates has purchased a 5.34 percent stake in Extended Stay,' which I thought was a good sign. I think it was last trading at 16. 'S&P announced it added Extended Stay to its Midcap 400 index.' If Extended Stay is getting added, then won't the mutual funds start buying it up? So wouldn't we want to buy it before all the mutual funds buy it and the price goes up?" She read a quote from George Dean Johnson in the press release lauding the move by S&P to include the stock in the Midcap 400, plus a Merrill Lynch note on the demand from mutual fund buyers. "George Dean referred to it as the Wal-Mart of hotels."

FROM DOLLARS TO DOUGHNUTS

"This could be another Krispy Kreme story," said one member, in reference to the confection maker based in Winston-Salem, North Carolina, which defied everyone with stock in fried dough that rose faster than yeasty bread. The women explained that a broker they knew had strongly advised them against Krispy Kreme. The company has long operated from a classic deco storefront on the main drag in Spartanburg. After decades in business, Krispy Kreme went public in 2000. The Piggy Bank Investments Club heeded the stay-away advice of the broker, who was simply parroting the widespread skepticism the food stock drew in the IPO market of tech darlings at the time. To the surprise of many, the IPO actually became one of the biggest high-fliers of the year. It doubled within a few weeks, and soon issued a two-for-one split. The success of Krispy Kreme irked the Piggy Bank members. Here was a local company—now with a stock market value of $2 billion—making good, and they hadn't even cashed in on it. "That's our biggest miss," said one member. Since then, the women are far more leery about heeding brokers' advice and underestimating local companies.

Georgia Anderson went upstairs to pull up Extended Stay's earnings information off the Internet and the group moved on to their next prospective stock, Pixar. Susan Jackson presented it. "You remember Pixar? They're the ones that have the animated films *Toy Story* and *A Bug's Life*. They're getting ready to bring out one called *Monsters Inc.*"

"Who did *Shrek*? That's the number-one movie."

"Dreamworks," offered someone else. "You can't buy stock in them, though."

"Pixar is down a little bit, not a whole lot, but it's gone down for the last five days," Jackson continued. "It's at 39.5. Its 52-week range is 25 to 46, give or take. Its P/E (profits to earnings ratio) is 33. I'll pass it around the chart. Of course, this is the one we should have bought. They've gone up 40 percent this year. Here we go again, have we missed this boat?" She read a news story on how the company raised its earnings forecast ahead of the release of *Monsters Inc.* The women thought it over.

"It's a gamble if *Monsters* is gonna be a great hit or not," Jackson concluded.

"Maybe what we ought to be doing is just looking at reviews of *Monsters*?"

"I know when *Toy Story* came out, I remember going to the movies with my daughter, and the line for *Toy Story* was out the building."

"Carol should have her boys evaluate *Monsters*."

"But if we wait for it to come out in November, we've missed it."

"That type of movie, I don't think you can go wrong with it."

The meeting was nearing a climax. The group needed to decide whether they were going to move ahead and buy a stock. Verizon, Merck, Pixar, and Extended Stay America were in the spotlight. Someone reminded the group that Piggy Bank owned Extended Stay in the past. Everyone started chatting about the price of the stock when the club bought it. No one recalled exactly how much the club made on it, but everyone figured they came out ahead. The conversation drifted a bit, then it was back to business.

"I think we oughta buy Extended Stay. I'm afraid this'll be another Krispy Kreme," said Bobbi Duncan. "I don't want that to happen again. We bought it before and we made money on it."

They ran through the pros: It's a local company, the stock is cheap; Bill Gates bought into it. With all the layoffs, maybe companies are bringing in more temporary workers. Construction workers stay there, and that sector is doing well. It's a member of the Midcap 400.

At that point, Mary Olejnik appeared after her son's Eagle Scout meeting. Warm greetings abounded. "I think I'd like a glass of wine," she said. Everybody laughed.

"We're contemplating buying Extended Stay," Jackson said.

"Again?" Olejnik asked from the kitchen. "Has it done anything since Bill Gates bought it?" She then mentioned the new Extended Stay headquarters that George Dean Johnson is building downtown. Everyone stopped to listen.

"I can tell you, the new building is going to be the Taj Mahal," Olejnik said.

"Is it really?" the others asked.

"It is absolutely gorgeous. They told the architects they wanted it to reflect the history of Spartanburg. And it has elements of Pine Street School, and two other old buildings downtown. It has five stories, three big fountains."

"Now I'm not sure I wanna buy the stock, if he's spending all that money on a corporate headquarters," said Jackson.

Olejnik chimed in again. "They're building more than they have been for a long time," she said. "Construction and men in the dog house are their bread and butter."

"When the economy gets worse, you'll have more men in the dog house," said Bobbi Duncan.

"There's a possibility that this could be a long, bad stretch like we had in the '70s," said Georgia Anderson. "There were people who got so sick of it that they got out of the market and never went back. There are a lot of amateurs who were investing who are getting weeded out in this kind of market."

"I hope it's not us," said Olejnik. "So many people—especially the young people who became tech millionaires—made the mistake of thinking that paper money was real. And it wasn't. When it was artificial to start with, the bubble had to burst. There are just some horror stories of people who were living beyond their inflated paper means, and now they're living on the poverty level."

"Well, what do you want to do?" Jackson said. "Should we sit and watch things? I'd be more than happy to watch Extended Stay. It's probably not gonna do much. We could wait it out for a couple of months."

"Well, we've been invited to a little gala at George's (George Dean Johnson's) house. I'll be chatting him up," said Olejnik.

"I'm wondering if we should buy a little bit," Jackson said.

"We could buy a little bit," another agreed.

The motion was made to buy about $3,200 worth of the Extended Stay stock.

It was the end of the evening and the women went home, with another successful meeting under their belt. They illustrate how the stock market can be what you make of it. For the Piggy Bank Investments Club, it's a bit of a social scene, a chance to hear about companies and perhaps grow their money. Chow down on some good eats. Over time, they learn more about how to come out ahead, and how to be careful with their money.

They didn't get in over their heads, they didn't push it, and they didn't day trade. They usually picked good stocks, and they had a hard time figuring out when to sell them. But even when times were tough, they hung in there and kept their money in the market. They weren't too greedy. They used whatever they could to make their stock-picking decisions, including research into how a store chain was doing, whether a movie released by a publicly traded company was successful, or how plans to build a company's headquarters were coming along.

They bought what they knew. They were not inclined to sell a stock right away on short-term bad news, which can be devastating for portfolios. Unlike hundreds of thousands of individual Americans who have machine-gun trigger fingers with their stocks, clubs like Piggy Bank were supported by their well-fed groups of regulars. They were more than likely to wait for the bounce back. Wall Street professionals, looking over their shoulders for the next freight-train wreck in the stock market, could use some of that kind of confidence and restraint.

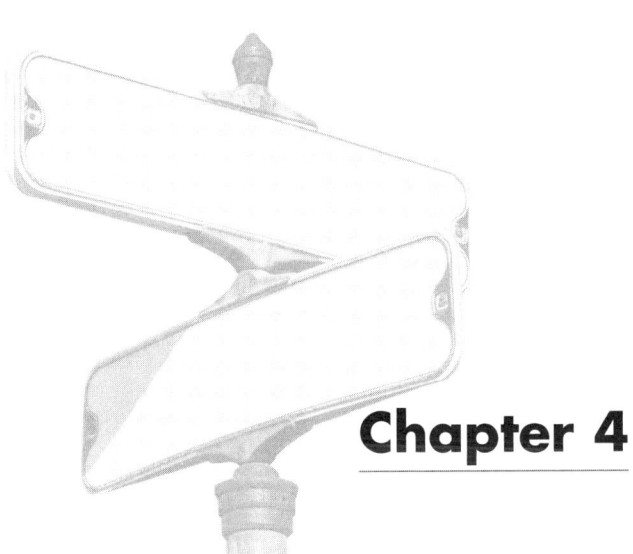

Chapter 4

The Pros Get Shattered but Fight Back

The Piggy Bank Investments, the No Cents Investment Club, and others from the ranks of millions of individual investors out there may seem harmless enough, but they represent a threat to the established players on Wall Street. As folks on Main Street pool their resources and focus their brains on stocks, the tug of war between the sellers and buyers of stock has intensified.

Legal battles and regulatory actions by the Securities and Exchange Commission (SEC) and Congress are mounting. The differences between the two sides—individual investors and professionals—didn't matter as much when everyone was making money, but in a bear market, the finger pointing starts and lawsuits follow. The gurus worshipped by individual investors saw their crystal balls shattered by the bear. Sell-side analysts came under increasing fire for conflicts of interest.

The most celebrated names on Wall Street were canned. In the middle of all this, the financial world had to climb back into the ring after getting its two front teeth knocked out in the World Trade Center terrorist attack of September 2001.

Since then, for Wall Street pro Liz Ann Sonders of Campbell Cowperthwait, it's more important than ever to arrive for battle at her midtown Manhattan office by 7 A.M. from her home in the executive suburb of Darien, Connecticut. She sits in her Wall Street command center, a corner office with a view of skyscrapers and the Hudson River. It's furnished with money-green carpeting, a desk, a small couch, and a couple of chairs, and decorated with pictures of her two-year-old son and three-year-old daughter. An American flag sits on her desk, along with flowers. Greeting visitors with a strong handshake, she unleashes a rapid-fire, no-nonsense speaking style honed from her years as a high-echelon player in the investment world. Tall and likeable in her fashion-forward print blouse, medium-length black skirt, and Prada heels, Sonders easily switches gears between stocks and dispensing parenting advice. "They don't eat when they get teeth," she explains when asked why babies seem to shun food at times. "My daughter hasn't eaten much in three days. She has huge molars in the top. Don't worry. Give her more milk. Put a little Ovaltine in it and some vitamins. Beef it up a little bit."

Over a bookcase hangs a picture of Louis Rukeyser, the silver-haired TV personality who hosted the PBS program *Wall Street Week*. Sonders has been a regular on the show and gets her picture on the program's website. The Excelsior Large Cap Growth Fund, trading under the ticker UMLGX, is a smallish $220 million mutual fund run by Sonders and the 30-person team at Campbell Cowperthwait, a money management unit of U.S. Trust, which in turn is an arm of discount brokerage giant Charles Schwab. About two thirds of the $3 billion managed by Campbell Cowperthwait comes from the firm's high net worth individuals with $2 million or more, or institutional customers with $5 million or more. For a $100,000 minimum, customers can open up a wrap account to access the firm's stock-picking prowess through participating brokers.

In late 2001, the Excelsior Large Cap Growth fund—aimed at mom-and-pop investors with less than $100,000 to invest—actually resembles the $30,000 joint account run by the Piggy Bank Investments Club of Spartanburg, South Carolina (see Chapter 3, "Savvy Southern Women Score"). The women counted 14 stocks in their portfolio. Sonders had 25. The Piggy Bank investors usually eyed big-name stocks from the S&P 500, which they would buy and hold for years at a time. Sonders's fund was fully invested—all the money was in stocks with none in money market accounts—and was composed of hefty companies with market caps of $5 billion or more with the expectation of holding them for three to five years. It was ranked in the 87th percentile by the Lipper Group, a company that tracks thousands of mutual funds. The score means only about 13 percent of the funds out there have outperformed it.

Yet even with the strong performance, Sonders is challenged. Retail investors are deciding to invest money on their own instead of buying a mutual fund managed by someone else. She doesn't mind people trading stocks on their own, but she argues that individuals should also own mutual funds as part of a balanced portfolio.

"Investors need to approach the stock market intellectually, not emotionally. Part of the way to do that is to get professional help," she says. "I just don't think an investment philosophy for an individual investor is to open an Ameritrade account and turn into a day trader. You need to have a plan. You need to understand your time horizon, your tolerance for risk, when you need the money, your ability to sleep at night, your need for income, what your goals are. Too few people have focused on all of those things."

Sonders rails against the John Bogle/Vanguard philosophy to pick a basket of stocks in the belief that passive investing has an edge over actively managed funds, partly because of lower fees. As of late 2001, some $1 trillion was invested in indexed stock market funds as Vanguard and its patriarch, Bogle, vied for supremacy against the actively managed mutual fund giant Fidelity.

"We make decisions based on fundamentals, not get forced into a name that has lousy fundamentals simply because it's 2 percent of the S&P 500 Index," Sonders argues. "It's just a different approach. Index funds in the '90s were the place to be. For a good eight years, index funds outperformed over 90 percent of all money managers. Passive outperformed active. A year and a half ago that reversed. I think we're going to go through a period of active outperforming passive. Usually it's a period of five to seven years."

Sonders hangs tough when asked about the Spartanburg, South Carolina, women's decision to purchase Extended Stay stock based partly on the size of the headquarters the company is building, backed up by gossip about the fancy homes executives in the firm are buying.

"That type of information is extremely valuable. It's sort of the Peter Lynch approach of buy what you know, buy what you understand. But it's not that simple. You can't invest based on what might seem to be blinding insight. Because there's a lot that goes on underneath the covers—balance sheet issues, income statement issues, investments the companies have, the management team, investment strategy. All of those things that are not as simple as going into a mall and saying, 'Hey, I see more people going into the Gap than I did last week, let's buy the stock.' That's definitely a component of it, but it has to go beyond that. The analysis has to go deeper than that, especially in the kind of market environment we're in right now."

Like other Wall Street pros, Sonders does field work to check out companies, products, and how they're performing with customers. The firm also carries a great deal of clout with prospective companies because its initial investment is 2 percent of Campbell Cowperthwait's total portfolio, or $60 million. That's a big enough chunk of money to draw the likes of General Electric CEO Jeff Immelt to meet personally with Sonders and others at the firm to pitch their company's stock. The access to big-name CEOs also boosts her knowledge-gathering process for her fund.

Sonders clearly wields more than the proverbial kitchen table used by mom-and-pop investors. She brandishes her wits, an MBA earned while working on Wall Street, and plenty of experience to help her navigate the tricky waters of the stock market. And she has an edge: insight into the closely guarded ranks of other fund managers from banks and institutions. While analysts on the sell-side are widely covered with their screaming upgrades and downgrades, the moves of the stock buyers on the other side of the aisle are harder to gauge. She boasts solid personal contacts in this arena to give her a better pulse on the market.

"I have a particularly unique sell-side, broker perspective since my husband runs sales at SoundView (a tech-flavored investment banking firm)," she points out. "His clients are all fellow money managers. So one of my unique sources of information is the people I've met through the media, as well as clients of my husband's. I probably know, more often than most, what other buy-side money managers are doing, which I think is helpful at times too."

For years Sonders has eaten, breathed, and slept stocks. She turns on CNBC at 5 A.M. when she wakes up, arrives at her desk by 7 A.M. each day after reading *The New York Times* and *The Wall Street Journal.* After checking the latest upgrades, downgrades, earnings, and mergers, she huddles with other senior staff each day to review strategy by the time the market opens at 9:30 A.M. She has two assistants at her disposal to help her track the market. And when she does make a move in her portfolio, she's backed by the consensus of a committee of the firm's best, brightest, and most powerful people. The process is not unlike what happens in meeting rooms of hundreds of money managers out there on Wall Street that handle trillions of dollars of investment money. They are the pros who the amateurs are trying to beat.

Yet with all these resources at her disposal, the net-asset value of the Excelsior Large Cap Growth Fund was down about 27 percent in 2001 after losing out on flagging companies like JDS Uniphase, the fiberoptics giant. Even the best and the brightest got sucked in. There was no place to hide. All stock sectors fell. In the words of Sonders's ex-boss, Wall Street pundit and fund manager Martin Zweig, author of *Winning on Wall Street*—you can't fight the tape. Saddled by dwindling profits and a cloudy economic picture, Sonders and most other Wall Street pros got pummeled in 2000 and 2001, even with stocks bravely rebounding from their lows in the final three months of 2001.

It certainly wasn't a good time to be a professional on Wall Street. Many of the most celebrated stock gurus hailed as the "wizards" in the 1990s turned out to be all too human when the curtain was lifted by the reality of the bursting bubble. Even the bears were too bullish. And the cheerleaders? They got shredded.

Ralph Acampora, chief technical analyst at Prudential Securities and one of the most celebrated bulls on Wall

Street, predicted his so-called "Fourth Megamarket" of big gains from 2000 to 2011. In fact, over the years, in some investment circles, he had earned the nickname Ralph "Make You Poorer" when his buoyant forecasts went bust.

Warren Buffett, the Sage of Omaha, has often touted index funds that follow the S&P 500 because "the know-nothing investor can actually outperform most investment professionals" this way. Unfortunately, the coveted S&P 500 gave up 10 percent in 2000 and 13 percent in 2001. Still, Buffett avoided the most bruising losses in the business by avoiding hyped-up technology and Internet stocks in favor of insurance investments and other so-called old-economy players.

Abby Joseph Cohen, the Goldman Sachs market strategist, predicted big gains in the early part of the new millennium, but her halo has seemed to fade somewhat in the face of profit warnings, economic woes, and withering returns. More recently, Cohen signaled her interest in small cap stocks, which have resisted some of the carnage. Is it a late call on a sector that will soon plummet? Only time will tell.

Peter Lynch, the white-haired founder of the Fidelity Magellen Fund and other widely held equity products, was often seen advising retail investors to taste the food and try products of companies in their portfolio in his overall buy-what-you-like mantra. During the bear market of 2001, his image was more scarce in the mutual fund firm's TV advertisements. His timing was impeccable.

John Bogle, the founder of Vanguard, marked the twenty-fifth anniversary of the Vanguard 500 with the nickname St. Jack. But even his motto of passive investing in indexes rather than betting on fund managers rings hollow in market conditions that shred all comers.

Two of the most widely quoted Internet analysts, Mary Meeker of Morgan Stanley and Henry Blodget of Merrill Lynch, went from "darlings" to "dogs" in a matter of months.

Meeker reportedly earned $15 million in 1999 when she hailed stocks like EBay and Amazon as the next big thing. For a while she was right, and then she came under fire. Reston, Virginia, Microsoft software salesman John Teeples entrusted stock options worth roughly $700,000 to Meeker's firm, Morgan Stanley, during the same time. Within 16 months, all that was left of his portfolio was $403.95 and a $40,000 tax bill. He filed an arbitration claim against his brokers in an attempt to get his money back. Meeker, at one point dubbed the "Internet Queen" as one of the most celebrated analysts on Wall Street, was also the subject of legal actions by shareholders of Amazon. com and EBay, accused of hyping companies with overly optimistic forecasts. A federal judge later dismissed eight cases against her saying they were abusive and based on market gossip. She remains at Morgan Stanley. No amended complaints were filed against her.

Blodget became famous in 1998 while at Oppenheimer when he issued a $400 price target for Amazon.com. Merrill Lynch soon hired him during the heyday of the Internet craze. His cheerleading continued with companies that soon went bust, such as Pets.com and EToys. In interviews with CBS MarketWatch, Blodget maintained that he always warned of risks in his stock reports and that along the way he never strayed from pointing out that 75 percent of all web companies would likely fail. In the summer of 2001, Merrill Lynch paid $400,000 to settle a claim by shareholders that Blodget's research contributed to their losses. By the fall of that year, Blodget announced he was leaving Merrill Lynch as part of an overall buyout offer extended to all the brokerage giant's employees. Even after all the carnage, *The Wall Street Journal* reported that Blodget walked away with a $2 million package.

The cases cast a spotlight on the investment banking industry. Some sell-side analysts or their firms would own shares of companies they covered, an apparent conflict of interest. Another cause of concern was the fact that investment banks would often court the companies they covered for lucrative investment banking work, such as handling mergers, acquisitions, and stock offerings. Members of Congress, who saw their portfolios shrink along with everyone else's, hastily called a round of hearings. Former Securities and Exchange Commission Chief Laura Unger testified that several analysts at undisclosed investment banks bought and sold stocks from their own personal accounts—against their own recommendations—and scored profits ranging from $100,000 to $3.5 million in the process.

The SEC issued guidelines to retail investors—ordinary folks—to look beyond analysts' ratings such as "buy" or "strong buy" and to research companies on their own. The recommendations included checking on whether a company's revenue was increasing, and whether lockup periods that restrict employee-owned shares might be ending. Another cause for concern: whether a bank participated in an initial public offering of a company. If so, the Wall Street bank had a vested interest in giving a glowing report on the company in an analyst report.

Even the term "analyst" is somewhat misleading. These people are indeed experts, but not neutral ones. They work for institutions that exist to make money. They're basically salespeople who sell stocks as products so their employers can pocket commissions in the process.

The industry is attempting to clean up its act as individual banks introduce policies that restrict analysts from owning stocks they cover. They're also trying to streamline the ratings system for companies, which investors find confusing. Chuck Hill, of Thomson Financial's First Call unit, which tracks analysts' ratings, complains that retail investors need a "secret decoder" when determining analyst ratings. In general, a "strong buy" or any other top rating by a bank means a company's stock price will grow 15 to 20 percent per year beyond the pace of the overall market. A plain "buy" reflects an expectation of 5 to 15 percent growth. A "hold," "neutral," or "market perform" rating means in line with the market. An "underperform" is 5 to 15 percent below the growth rate of the overall market. "Sell" implies the stock could lose as much as 20 percent. Only about 1 percent of all companies carry the dreaded "sell" rating, despite the overall bear market conditions. That's partly because analysts won't cover a company in the first place if they don't feel they can build a compelling reason to buy it. Plus, a "sell" recommendation would usually hamper any effort by analysts to get access to the company.

The tug of war between pros and individual stock investors took a turn toward the latter with the implementation of regulation Full Disclosure (Reg FD). Introduced by Arthur Levitt, the former chief of the SEC, Reg FD requires companies to disclose key financial information in a more public way through press releases or other public statements, rather than the old way of telling favorite Wall Street analysts first. Although it's difficult to enforce, it has helped level the playing field and break up the "old boy" network between companies and analysts. Nevertheless, many individual investors remain distrustful of financial institutions and prefer to go it alone. Other investors still prefer to have financial institutions watch their money for them.

SEPTEMBER 11, 2001

The contentiousness between individuals and pros was knocked off the public agenda for a while by the September 11 terrorist attacks. Money issues took a back seat to raw survival, especially on Wall Street. Consider that the World Trade Center comprised a big share of office space in Manhattan's Financial District, and that it also included a mammoth shopping mall. It was also one of the busiest transportation hubs in the country with the convergence of subway and PATH trains from New Jersey, plus ferry and bus services nearby. The 14-acre site of what became known as Ground Zero also contained vital infrastructure links for all of lower Manhattan.

Firms Cantor Fitzgerald and Marsh & McLennan lost hundreds of employees among the roughly 3,000 who died in the disaster at the World Trade Center. The New York Stock Exchange closed for four days, then managed to reopen.

Lehman Brothers was one of many Wall Street firms forced to move. The company rapidly leased an entire 650-room Sheraton hotel in midtown Manhattan to temporarily house its investment banking unit. Mattresses were stacked up on the sidewalk and desks brought in. Within days, they were up and running. Lehman moved its lucrative bond trading business from the 38th, 39th, and 40th floors of the demolished World Trade Center across the Hudson River to a backup site in Jersey City, New Jersey. This site had been prepared during jitters surrounding the Year 2000 computer bug.

People put behind them the images of monstrous clouds of smoke and debris raining down on employees and rescue workers. They rolled up their sleeves and got the wheels of business turning again. It was the best way to fight back, people collectively decided. When employees showed up for the first few days in Jersey City after Wall Street reopened on September 17, Lehman bought them lunch the entire week in the company cafeteria. Phone numbers were posted for an employee assistance hotline. Lehman knocked down panels between office cubicles so salespeople could see each other in the mode of a classic, open trading room floor. A few days later, TV monitors were hung from the ceiling and tuned to financial channels. Downstairs in the lobby, hundreds of employees streamed in and out to pick up food to eat at their desks. A 7-by-10-foot American flag hung on the wall by the front door. A couple of guys walked by wearing T-shirts that read, "I'm bullish on America." A makeshift security checkpoint consisting of a table, security guards, and a jury-rigged telephone blocked entry to the upper floors. Impatient visitors waited to get clearance to go upstairs. Despite the crowded conditions and long waits for elevators, employees coped. Lehman started floating billions of dollars in bond deals within days of the disaster.

When the planes hit the World Trade Center, Campbell Cowperthwait's Liz Ann Sonders was sitting on a runway at Newark Airport, the same point of origin as one of the four hijacked planes in the attack. "It could just as well have been me on one of those planes," she said. Although shaken by the experience, she came back to work later that week while the city was mostly shut down and the stock market was closed. "You kind of felt like you wanted to come to New York to work. A lot of people were afraid, but I felt like, 'Screw you, I'm coming to New York. I'm gonna walk down these streets that I love.'"

Life on Wall Street went on in the face of the disaster and the war on terrorism. Campbell Cowperthwait trimmed its holdings in Home Depot in the face of rising competition from rival Lowe's. The firm held on to insurer AIG in the belief that the September 11 disaster would weed out weaker players and give dominant companies more market share and pricing power. "We're big into management teams and they have a strong lineup," Sonders said.

In 2002, Sonders continues to like health care in general, particularly sector leader Pfizer. She's also holding on to media company AOL Time Warner because of "their combination of technology and content, and owning the distribution system of the content." She touts motorcycle company Harley-Davidson as "the consummate brand." In 2001, the firm took a position in mortgage specialist Freddie Mac because it's done well in a tough market environment, "plus there's still a lot of wind at their back" as more home owners refinance to take advantage of lower interest rates.

Sonders agrees that analysts at Wall Street brokerages continue to suffer from image problems. The company's wrap program of providing access to fund managers for a minimum of $100,000 is aimed at removing broker recommendations from the picture and thereby reducing possible conflicts between individuals and institutions.

As corporate earnings dwindled and layoffs mounted, Sonders kept a brave face as she looked into 2002. "There's still not a lot of visibility, although there are enough companies that have come out and suggested they may have seen a bottoming even if the rebound off of that isn't stellar over the next quarter or two. That's enough good news in this environment right now. That's what investors are looking for." Gone are the days where individual investors expect to see exceptional earnings growth from companies. Hearing things are not going to get worse is a strong positive, she points out.

Whether the market snaps back into another boom remains to be seen, and with the war on terrorism and the Enron bankruptcy scandal in the headlines, almost anything can happen. While individual investors and institutions continue to have their differences, everybody welcomes a bottom of the bear market, if this is it. Sonders remains upbeat. "There is an awesome set of statistics that points toward pervasive pessimism right now, which is the cornerstone to a view of the market not being so bad." In other words, when it's as dark as it can be, the dawn may not be far off.

During the boom, the pros seemed like geniuses. But even they can't read the future. Wall Street's analysts published plenty of disclaimers saying exactly this during the boom of 1996 to early 2000. Alas, few were listening. When stocks went down, all of a sudden the pros all became schmucks. Conflicts in the financial services industry remain, and attempts at reform are continuing in Washington and within the industry itself. Mom-and-pop investors will continue to use brokers, buy mutual funds and index funds, and read analysts' reports. But there's one trend that Wall Street, in the wake of the new century's financial upheavals, can't stop. A growing number of ordinary folks in America will begin to make their own calls on cheap or expensive stocks. The hungriest investors will be more inclined to check a company's bottom line and do a little sniffing around on their own.

As Yale Hirsch, founding editor of Wall Street's yearly guidebook *Stock Trader's Almanac,* once said, "If you don't profit from your investment mistakes, someone else will."

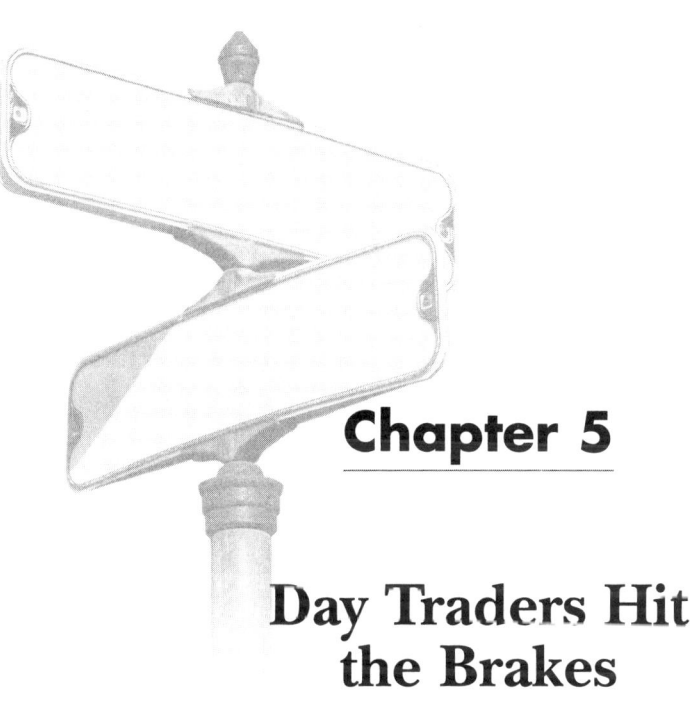

Chapter 5

Day Traders Hit the Brakes

There's a saying by race car driver Mario Andretti that if you feel like you're in control, you're probably not going fast enough. The remark is relevant to the most obsessive of all individual stock market investors, namely, the furious and fast day traders. Race car drivers work alone when they're behind the wheel. So do most day traders—people who buy and sell the same stocks multiple times each day. The ranks of both are made up mostly of men and some women who love speed, danger, and the thrill of the race as they plummet down the track, riding the barrier between raw speed and brushes with death.

Just as Indy 500 race cars deploy the latest technology, day traders rev up web connections that execute trades with the speed of a checkered flag flapping in a 200-mile-per-hour slipstream. While investment clubs represent the slower boats in the armada of Americans in the stock market, day traders are the most manic, the most risky, and by far the most complex. By some estimates, day traders account for almost half of all online trading by individual Americans. The day-tripper's influence on stock prices, mostly in the fast-moving Nasdaq stock market, often confounds the large Wall Street banks, and government regulators too.

Wall Street is what you make of it. That's been the central theme of financial markets since day one. If you want to wade in to your ankles like many investment clubs do with monthly stock picks and buy-and-hold strategies, that's fine. But it doesn't work for the loners of the stock market. Day traders swim in the deepest, choppiest, and murkiest waters outside of the safe harbor of buy and hold. They short stocks, they buy options, they trade currency, or do whatever they can to make a buck. Complex machinations used by the most sophisticated hedge funds are their bread and butter. As a day trader, the only limitations are your own intellect to grasp the countless transactions and your knowledge of the markets. This is inherently frustrating because you can never know too much.

There's plenty of danger out there, too. Seeking bigger payoffs, day traders, like the lone gunman fleeing a bail bondsman, often end up owing their brokers money if they bet on stocks to go down by shorting them, but then shares go up. Margin purchases, where investors borrow up to 50 percent of the value of their portfolios from a broker to buy stocks, can also be costly. If the value of the client's portfolio falls—as many did during periods of meltdown in 2000 to 2002—brokers can demand cash to cover their loan, or sell off stocks in the customer's portfolio. Another dangerous area is penny stocks or other thinly traded shares that can make big moves on low volume. This is the territory of many day traders who post messages on bulletin boards in an attempt to sway the stock price. Sometimes it works.

There is no widely recognized umbrella group or trade association for day traders, nor is there a licensing body. They are not brokers in the institutional sense of the word. All they need is a computer, a web connection, and various software tools and services to trade stocks and track the market. The barriers to entry are small, but the hurdles to making money at it nowadays are much higher. It's hard to know exactly how many day traders exist out there on the racetrack, but they leave tire marks all over the market. Some estimates put them as high as 200,000 or more during the Nasdaq bubble, including 10,000 to 20,000 higher rollers. During the '90s, day traders burned up volume for online trading firms such as Charles Schwab, TD Waterhouse, and ETrade. They helped raise the fortunes of market makers such as Knight Trading Group. They grabbed plenty of headlines as the wheelers and dealers of the new economy, known for trading in and out of stocks several times a minute to capture small gains at a time, in order to quickly build up big profits.

In 2002, things have been much quieter. Trading volumes at online brokers are way down, and everyone says there are fewer day traders around. Ken Calhoun of DayTrading University.com, a website for day trading entrepreneurs, estimates about 18,000 day traders are plying the market for profits nowadays.

TOKYO JOE

For quintessential day trader "Tokyo Joe" Park, the stock swoon of the early twenty-first century has taken a bite out of subscribers to his "Societe Anonyme" e-mail service and newsletter. The ranks of the $200-per-month members have dwindled from a peak of 4,000 to about 900 in early 2002. Still, membership has climbed from its low of about 600 in 2001. Even with the lower number, Park still pulls in about

$160,000 a month on his newsletter alone, which is more than enough to help run his day-trading business and employ five. While things have slowed down, Tokyo Joe still trades like crazy to make more money. The motto on Park's TokyoJoe.com website reads, "Throw out 10 lines, catch one whale." The 51-year-old Korean-born lawyer, less known by his formal name of Yun Soo Oh Park, poses in a photo on his website with chiseled chin, tiny dark glasses, and upward gaze. Nearby are images of his villa in southern France and a Lamborghini Diablo Roadster. ("Cars are just little toys," he later explains.)

There are those who think Tokyo Joe is something of a crook. The Securities and Exchange Commission settled a civil fraud suit against him for $750,000 after charging he dumped shares he owned while telling his subscribers to buy without disclosing his ownership or plans to sell. Tokyo Joe maintains he did nothing different than the leading brokerage firms on Wall Street with their various conflicts of interest—leveraging their sell-side analysts to flog stocks while pocketing commissions and lining up sweet investment banking deals from the same companies.

"The SEC said I was front running. Who does not front run? They pump because they have a vested interest," says Tokyo Joe. With an upbeat persona that shrugs off the toughest questions, he dismisses institutional investors as the real bad guys. "We short stocks all the time—Q-Logic, Juniper. We play where the market is going for the day. We don't listen to Goldman Sachs and Lehman and all those vested-interest assholes. They're the scum of the earth."

CBS MarketWatch editor-in-chief Thom Calandra recalled the first time he met Park, at one of those small-investor money shows in London. "The Nasdaq was getting hammered and there were plenty of reports about this guy's notoriety and his problems with the SEC," recalls Calandra. "Most of the established financial commentators, the stuffed shirts, were steering clear of him. Time comes for Joe's speech, and the crowds flocked to the guy. They were hanging on every word he said. Tokyo Joe is blasphemous, he's cocky. But he knows how to make ordinary folks feel powerful." Tokyo Joe has changed his ways a bit. Besides paying the SEC settlement, which admits no wrongdoing on his part in a standard pact with the regulatory agency, he now discloses his holdings on his website so investors can see what axes he's grinding at the moment. He also runs a three-page disclaimer "so no one can mess with me." The document points out his role as an independent source for momentum investors on stocks that have investment potential, but that none of the statements "are meant to be a solicitation or recommendation to buy." For now, however, Tokyo Joe is focused on doing what he does best—following the market and spending and making money, and coming up with antics that involve both.

 Born in Seoul to parents of Korean and Japanese descent, Tokyo Joe speaks languages from both sides of his family as well as French, Arabic, Spanish, and of course, English. As a teenager he ran away to Mexico to study painting and ended up serving time in a Mexican jail for entering the country illegally. He played it straight after that, returning home and attending law school in Japan, before moving on to an attorney's job at Hyundai Group, where he worked for 14 years. His tour of duty included stints in Seoul, Tokyo, Düsseldorf, Paris, Monte Carlo, and London, spending an entertainment budget of up to $500,000 per year. "My job was taking care of problems, wherever they happened," he once said. "You think investing is tough, try suing Quaddaffi." He traces the nickname Tokyo Joe to London in 1981, when a nightclub called Tokyo Joe opened. Perhaps the bar was named after a 1949 Humphrey Bogart film of the same name, but at any rate, Tokyo Joe showed up on the first night, wearing too many gold chains around his neck. The next day, when the

London Times wrote a review of the club and said it was full of foreigners wearing gold chains, his friends started calling him Tokyo Joe. The name stuck.

Fed up with life abroad, Tokyo Joe negotiated a severance deal and came to New York with his wife and daughter. He bought a loft in New York City near the United Nations, and started playing the stock market on his own. He bought three Mexican restaurants, and closed two, while plotting his moves from behind the cash register through an account from Merrill Lynch. Discontent with the service, he bought a PC and a modem and discovered the Internet. On Internet chat sites like The Motley Fool, he registered his handle as TokyoMex, in reference to his restaurants. He became famous for prolific and insightful commentary on the market, laced with recipes of life. One early posting in December 1996 dispenses travel advice on Egypt: "Walk around with belly sucked in, not in a Nike and not with a stupid Kodak dangling from your wrist. Dress up like the Casablanca and wear a Panama." Tokyo Joe almost gets poetic during a trip to Egypt in which he rented an ancient sailboat called a dhow:

"My boatsman Ali in his 40s and Yagoub had their cooking pots, tea boilers, and an array of provisions including dates and nuts. Spend two days exploring the area then catch the downstream flow and head north to Luxor, Thebes, Valley of the Kings, and all along the way you will pass villages, farmers, and less known cities of the past. Yagoub will wash your shirt every day in the Nile and hang it up on the mast (so) it would be fresh next day as largest golden sun rises in mist of moisture from surrounding greenery near the Nile. Children will be standing by the shore line and wave their hands, 'Salam, Salam,' and as you (round a) bend the village from the minarets (you hear) the chanting of the morning wake up Sallah, ah ah ah ah ah … ah aaaaaa. Allah Akbar. It is the most heart-wrenching sound to hear that will take you back instantly to the middle of the desert of the olden days when the Saracens traversed these deserts all the way to Cote Ivor to bring back slaves to Makka."

His postings also included philosophies on life itself, and the stock market.

"I don't do this only for the money, I have money," he said. "I have family money before this, but I never touch it! I cannot stand bourgeois assholes who are so into their measly 20 to 30 percent gains regardless of humanity and values. That's why I'm willing to get all over these assholes who are hyping stocks online. You have to have a life. You have to have fun and know what (is) important in life."

Yet hyping stocks is exactly what some say he did himself when setting up his own newsletter subscription business under the name Tokyo Joe. Of course Tokyo Joe says he cares more about floating down the Nile than money, but nevertheless, the man could day trade with the best of them.

In one case in late 1998, an analyst at S&P told Money.com that he noticed strange behavior in a stock he was following, FileNet. Shares of the maker of document software jumped $3, or about 40 percent, to $11 on volume of 3.5 million shares, double the norm. Yet there was no news on the stock. Checking the message board, Silicon Investor, the analyst found the culprit. Tokyo Joe had announced he liked the stock and expected it to go higher. It did.

Another famous Tokyo Joe stock was Iomega, the computer storage company that soared, then crashed as he took part in hyping it on the message boards. Tokyo Joe developed a following as one of the most talked-about traders on the web, and like other day trader pundits, he turned it into his own cottage industry. Starting out with an e-mail list of some 2,000 devotees, he began charging people for his advice. Setting up his own chat room, Tokyo Joe tracked the market by the second, occasionally hearing information on stocks. He once acted on a rumor from one of his members that J.C. Penney would make a bid to buy Genovese Drug. He bought Genovese at $25.25 and sold it at $31 within four days.

Karen Kosoy, also known as TMFKaren, runs a chat room on The Motley Fool. She recalled Tokyo Joe's heyday, but said he'd been absent from the message board scene once his own business took off. "I haven't been in touch with, or followed, Tokyo Joe for many years. If I had anything to say, it would be that he was a pioneer in active Internet stock trading, but eventually, his popularity bit him in his tush!"

The party had to end sometime. In September 2000, the SEC sued the well-known Internet stock guru. The SEC charged that Park pocketed fees from his readers of more than $1.1 million from July 1998 to June 1999. He allegedly failed to disclose the tips were on stock he already owned, while selling the same stocks. In a practice the industry dubs "scalping," he pocketed profits by selling the stock into the buying flurry he created. He repaid $324,934 in gains and a fine of $429,696 to the SEC and went back to work, sending out 40 to 50 e-mails a day to his customers. Tokyo Joe claims he earns a trading profit of $5,000 per day by making 60 to 100 trades and betting with as much as $6 million. He needs to make big money to handle his $500-per-hour lawyer fees, he joked. But he's aware of the bear market's toll. "I know a diamond merchant on 47th Street (in New York) who lost $187 million on stocks," he said.

After all the hardships around him, Tokyo Joe is still living large on the East Side of Manhattan. "I start trading before the bell. After the bell, I drink like crazy," he said as he spoke on his cell phone and received a back rub. "You're not going to be able to stop by today?" he asked a caller with a hint of disappointment. "I was going to take you to a Geisha house," he added, in reference to the Japanese institutions that offer worldly women for entertainment and enlightenment.

When the World Trade Center was attacked, Tokyo Joe saw a chance to jump into the market again. "Buy when Paris is burning," he said. "We bought on September 23, GE, AOL, Nokia." Cashing out by the end of each trading day and going long on only a handful of stocks, Tokyo Joe headed into 2002 focusing on "Bin Laden plays," stocks getting boosted by the war against terrorism, such as facial recognition software maker Visionics and InVision Technologies. Tokyo Joe bought InVision at $5.50 and watched it climb to nearly $50 per share. He shorted Enron at 32, but then covered it at 20 instead of riding it down all the way. He still made money on the bankrupt energy trading firm, perhaps the biggest Wall Street flameout of all time.

Tokyo Joe still gets press despite the passing of the bull market and his brush with the law. "I like to show them that anybody can do this. You don't have to have a Ph.D. It's common sense. I'm all self-taught. I'm a Horatio Alger story. An Internet pundit." He maintains that his biggest weapon against naysayers is his own material success. "I want to have as many toys as possible. The best revenge is having the most toys. I would also like to help people who are disadvantaged. I have a charity section on my web page. I like fine art. I like sculpture. That's my passion, collecting art. I like traveling. Cars are just a little toy."

Even if one believes everything Tokyo Joe says about how much money he makes, rank-and-file day traders are riding a rougher stretch of track nowadays. Seven of 10 day traders lose money by the end of a typical day, by some estimates. After all, someone has to lose in order for others to profit, as the law of averages dictates. While people were forgetting this lesson during the bubble, some sobering stuff happened as a grim reminder of the dark side of the stock market. In August of 1999, Mark Barton, a chemist turned day trader, went into a murderous rage after losing about $500,000 on the market. He shot nine people at two brokerage firms in Atlanta before killing himself.

The shooting put day traders on edge and prompted the SEC to pass a rule requiring disclosure statements outlining the risks of day trading to clients. "You should not fund day trading activities with retirement savings, student loans, second mortgages, emergency funds, funds set aside for purposes such as education or home ownership, or funds required to meet your living expenses," the new rule says. The SEC also passed a $25,000 margin rule, which puts a higher cash requirement on day traders. To do more than four buy-and-sell transactions on a stock in a week, the rule stipulates, you must have at least $25,000 in your account.

A much more sober environment pervades nowadays overall, says Ken Calhoun of DayTradingUniversity.com, an education site for day traders. He estimates about 15,000 to 18,000 day traders are out there, from a survey he'd seen. A former statistician and quality control specialist for Ford, Calhoun turned to stock trading more heavily in the late '90s and then launched his training website because of demand for education "beyond the fluff out there." Although his membership dropped about 20 percent to 2,800 during the bear market, his website continues to cater to people who have tried and lost on the market, or people who have read how-to books but want to learn more about how intraday trading works.

Calhoun provides technical analysis on risk management with a specialty in intraday trades of 2 to 10 minutes in duration. Even with all his intellectual firepower, it still took him about two years just to break even. "I'm a UCLA grad, with all these credentials, yet it took a lot of practice and hard work. Most people get killed. They don't have the time or the patience." Starting with a single PC and an account with Datek, Calhoun now uses six monitors and eSignal, a real-time stock ticker service, to follow each individual trade on a stock. "You have to have the right tools and know how to use them," he explains.

While Calhoun has never had a run-in with the SEC in the vein of Tokyo Joe, he did speak with the regulatory agency at one time about the practice of posting hypothetical performance results, which falls within a gray area of the law. He avoids hyping at any cost. "I don't tout stocks. I use examples, mostly on software, semiconductor, and biotech stocks." Living in Hawaii, he has to get up at 3 A.M. or earlier to follow the opening bell in New York, which is six hours ahead. He drinks a pot of coffee, and off he goes.

He sets up two-day charts with two-minute candle sticks, which are graphic illustrations that show upward and downward price moves. When a stock is losing momentum from the previous day, it's a short candidate. If it's high over the previous day, he may go long. His method involves decoding the buy-and-sell triggers from the bigger fish, namely institutions. By tracking moves on a minute-by-minute basis, Calhoun can trade on the money flow and fair value of stocks at the moment, just ahead of upward or downward changes. "Charts are what you should trust and not the analysts. That would have saved people billions," he says. "Nowadays, day traders are more serious. There are a lot of ways to lose. They've walked through land mines. ... You don't see as many young kids, or foolish people."

Ray Johns, director/CEO of DayTraders.com, says nearly 90,000 people tried his day-trading service between 1996 and 1999 during the height of the bull market. It reminds him of

Japan in the '80s, when the Nikkei went so high it was hard to get anything done. People figured they could make $5,000 a day on the market rather than going to their jobs during the Internet bubble in the U.S. "We got e-mail from people who said they were quitting their jobs and day trading their mortgages. We got some real weird ones. People said they ran up their credit cards and college money and became millionaires. People found out that the stock market is not really a nice place. It doesn't mind taking your money if you don't know what you're doing. Investing is not just a road to riches, it's a difficult way to make a living. People found out it wasn't easy, and lost money. And they hung up their hat."

But when the market levels and the economy improves down the line, people will inevitably come back. "The lesson is, it's not as easy as it looks," Johns says. "If you're gonna be a day trader, you've got to be willing to change on a dime and willing to go short, as you were long. Psychologically it's hard for people to short the market. You've got to be able to stand back and take in the fundamentals, and the economy, and the emotional state of people overpaying."

MAKING A HOBBY OF IT

Besides the self-employed, crazy day traders, there are plenty of other solo players out there in the stock market. These are the hobbyists, people who usually act on their own, who play the market as amateur day traders, gambling with a reasonable amount of money. It's as good a pastime as collecting stamps, and it can be more exciting in some ways. You set aside a few thousand to play the market, you buy stocks, you sell stocks, you follow the business news, you complain to everyone about it, you swap theories and war stories. Maybe you earn enough to buy a sailboat. Some actually get good enough at it to make a living, if that's what they want to do.

To Rupert Jee, tech stocks are like turkey and roast beef, his favorite sandwich ingredients. In 2001, the owner of the Hello Deli in New York City was day trading from a laptop behind his cash register while filling food orders and ringing up his receipts. The multi-tasking egg house proprietor never wavered from his love of his Nasdaq beauties: Cisco, Applied Micro, Sycamore Networks, and many others, despite the bear market. In the past, Jee has made real gravy from his tech stocks, but his meat-and-potatoes money comes from his shop, which possesses the magic three-word formula for success: location, location, location. It's situated next to the Ed Sullivan theater in Times Square.

When David Letterman moved to the block in the early '90s, the locale was one of the more neglected corners of the theater district, way up on 53rd Street. Now the block is flooded with star-struck tourists who work up a big hunger from standing in line for tickets to *The Late Show*. Over the years, Letterman has roped many of the shopkeepers on his block into live TV gags, and Rupert Jee has been one of the stars. He figures he's been on TV with Letterman about 100 times. "He'd get me wired up and they'd be in a van," he says. "Letterman would get me to say things. People called the cops on me a number of times and I made a woman cry once." One of his favorite routines was posing as a waiter and sticking his thumb into a glass of water in front of some women, then feigning ignorance when they complained.

Tapping into the memorabilia of the neighborhood, Jee offers sandwiches named after celebrities. There's a Paul Shaffer for *The Late Show* music director; and of course, the Letterman: turkey, ham, American cheese, lettuce, tomato, sweet peppers, mayo, oil, and plenty of vinegar. Celebrity photos of Raquel Welch, Wynonna Judd, Charlie Sheen, and many others hang on the wall, and Jee plays up his Letterman appearances with a sign in the front window that reads "As Seen on TV" in fat red letters.

In 2001, his tourist customers would ask him about Letterman, while his regular customers would joke with him about the stock market. "He's got a buy order in one hand and a deli sandwich in the other," said one regular. Another walked in and lamented about his shares of Lucent before ordering a cup of coffee. "I still believe in technology. It's the future," Jee said then. He admitted that it's hard to take orders and buy stocks at the same time, but he does his best. "One time I bought some shares of a stock and planned to sell it, but then I got a breakfast rush and the stock dropped out on me."

For Michail Shadkin, 39, of Florida, day trading started out as a hobby, but in 2000, he did so well he started doing it full time. That was the year he won $1 million in the Ameritrade Investors Cup after ringing up huge gains in the virtual stock-picking contest, another passion of wannabe day traders. Starting during bear market conditions with a $50,000 mock portfolio, Shadkin ballooned his holdings up to $328,140 in a month after a series of 155 transactions. "You gotta buy the champs and short the chumps" is his mantra. When he wasn't entering contests, Shadkin day traded from home, spending about seven hours a day doing stock research and a half-hour trading from his online account. He was a true solo player who checked up on what the experts said, but acted alone. "Wall Street analysts come out with their buy ratings too late and their sell ratings too late. Do not listen to them. Don't buy the hype. Do your own research." His method was to find weak companies, wait for their stocks to get a boost from any positive news, short the stock, and then sell the options within 30 days when the stocks went back down again. "I read everything, I manage my own accounts, and I spend a lot of time in the house with my wife and my son. It's a great life."

David McCuistion, 27, a software developer at Helm Software in Tempe, Arizona, began blending his technical expertise with his stock picking in 2001. He first got interested in the stock market after college, when he bought a car and realized how he'd messed up his credit. "I started devouring personal finance books and websites, which of course led me to think of investing," he says. He devised software of his own making that searches Nasdaq stocks and eliminates stocks that are too cheap or with low volume because they're prone to wild swings. McCuistion's computer code analyzes the remaining stocks and compares factors like recent price performance, trading volume, moving averages, industry movements, and index movements. It selects stocks to short if the market is heading down, and stocks to buy if the market looks bullish. "Basically it's a momentum system, with some tweaks. I think this is what a lot of other people are doing, but they're doing it by hand or with an off-the-shelf software package, and it's all about the tweaks and fine tuning." McCuistion's strategy as of 2001 was to invest only a portion of his savings and use the software mostly for stock-picking competitions. Most of his money was in market index funds like Spyders and Cubes—which represent entire classes of Standard & Poor's 500 and the Nasdaq 100 Index.

"I don't like the idea of investing in single companies based on their fundamentals," McCuistion said. "Investing is more like playing a game of numbers rather than building a business. It's more like blackjack, where the individual cards are effectively random but where you can take advantage of the game by placing large bets at certain times that are more likely than usual to produce the desired result."

He devised another method that successfully beefed up his girlfriend's savings to buy a new car. Using the Java programming language, he deployed a Linux server using a MySQL (an open source, structured query language) database. The system gathered data from the websites of Yahoo!, Nasdaq, and Standard & Poor's. He would switch investments weekly between Spyders, Cubes, and Diamonds, based on recent price performance, long-term moving averages, trading volume, and market action. "I did reasonably well, but I was managing my beautiful girlfriend's investments with this system and she needed her money to buy a car. I later felt guilty about putting her car money at risk with an unproven system, but not that guilty." In 2002, he took all his money out of the market to make a down payment on a house. Lately, he's been eyeing strategies that use fewer trades and other metrics. "As soon as my house is built and I've saved a bit of dough, I'll be back at it."

In mid 2001, 34-year-old Seattle resident Peter Anthony Bjornerud believed in buying on fear and selling on greed. The self-employed day trader touted himself as a contrarian, defined by Webster's as "an investor who makes decisions that contradict prevailing wisdom." The former bartender and disc jockey also saw himself as something of a propeller head, which is an affectionate term for slightly geeky folks who excel at numbers. For his persona online, Bjornerud adopted the name Quisp, a brand of breakfast cereal from the 1970s that has enjoyed a minor revival on the Internet. Quisp is a space alien with a propeller head and wild eyes, a good icon for any day trader. Bjornerud believed in selling stock when analysts upgraded and buying when they downgraded. He grew up in Seattle and went to school in England. Around 1996, his brother gave him $10,000 to start trading. He nearly lost the whole pot, down to $900. At that point, he became a student of the market, scouring corporate results, technical data, and income statements posted on the Internet.

Becoming known in chat rooms and community sites such as Clearstation, Raging Bull, and StockJungle, Bjornerud published a newsletter that featured "Q-Tips." At one point, he claimed 1,200 subscribers, but closed the newsletter after the Tokyo Joe scandal in 2000. A former bartender at Aubergine, a swanky restaurant in Seattle run by Wolfgang Puck, he was once the host of an electronic music show at the University of Washington's radio station, KCMU. In his apartment he kept a turntable near his trading desk, which was packed with monitors. Bjornerud says the best traders are musicians and mathematicians, but you can't discount the value of research. "Everybody who invests in stocks should at least know something," he says. Another of his rules: "When there's a lot on the line and your stock is falling, you can't get emotional."

These solo players are a bit like lone gunmen, not in the killer sense, but more in the vein of the Old West. They ride their silicon horses over the peaks and valleys, scouting for the next bonanza. When that payoff will come, nobody really knows for sure. Not even, he admits freely, Tokyo Joe.

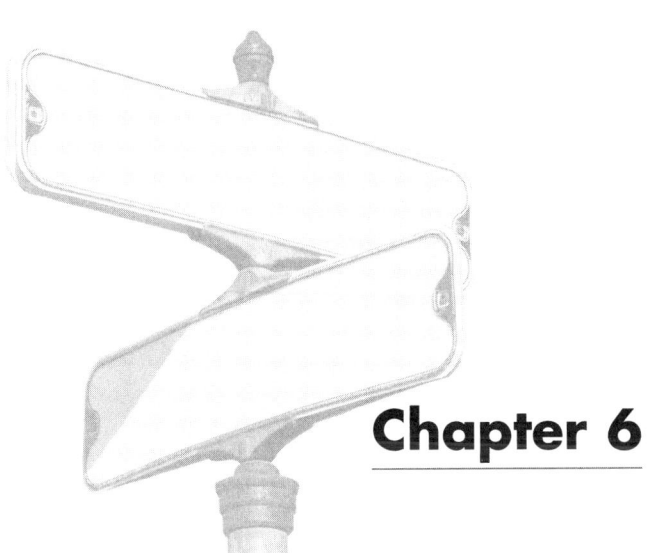

Chapter 6

African Americans Invest in Community

Richmond, the capital of Virginia, is the source of some major money flows toward Wall Street—from the likes of James River paper company, tobacco giant Philip Morris, Ethyl Corporation, Reynolds Aluminum, and Circuit City. These are mighty companies with big payrolls and scions of industry at their helms. The Gottwald family, owners of a big chunk of chemical firm Ethyl, and the Ukrops supermarket magnates often come up in conversations about Richmond's wealthiest residents. One of the most famous icons of the city is the late tennis pro Arthur Ashe. A statue in his likeness now stands in a famous promenade in town, Monument Avenue, with the inscription "Since we are surrounded by so great a cloud of witnesses, let us lay aside every weight and the sin which so easily ensnares us, and let us run with endurance the race that is set before us." Those are inspiring words indeed, especially for those who brave the stock market nowadays.

So much money is generated in and around Richmond, the Federal Reserve uses the city as the center of one of its 12 districts in the U.S. Richmond is headquarters for district five, which covers Maryland, the District of Columbia, Virginia, West Virginia, North Carolina, and South Carolina. Banking is a big part of the city overall, as a transfer point for investments in the stock market and elsewhere.

Back in the early 1990s, Carolyn Robinson had finished high school and was working in the trust department at one of the big banks. While keeping the area's investment machinery running for the city's wealthy residents as they ferried money over to Wall Street, she began to think about her own financial future. "I literally touched millions of dollars of trades per day," Robinson said. "I wanted a piece of this, I thought at the time. But I had all the misconceptions, like you need a lot of money. I didn't understand how the market works." Although she did invest in a 401(k) from an employer, as an African American the stock market was relatively new to her. "I had no exposure to the market at all as a child. That was something we did not discuss in our household. I was reared by my great-grandparents in a rural area, so (investing in the stock market) was just something that black folks didn't do. I learned about the basics, (having) savings and life insurance, which is a foundation before you can go to the next level, but that's as much as I got at home."

Along with her co-worker Adrienne Whitaker, Robinson started scouring books and magazines about the stock market. Whitaker brought in an article in *Black Enterprise* magazine about a family that started an investment club and made millions. Up until then, the two friends hadn't even heard of an investment club. Whitaker had made it through college without much thought beyond basic business courses, but the women figured it was time to make a move. At first they thought they'd start something up with their respective families, but everyone was scattered around the country. So they decided to form Investors 2000 with themselves and a few close friends. This was 1993, well before the Internet or the stock bubble of the decade really took off. But even without a lot of hype coming from the overall market, it wasn't hard to find other members.

Meeting to discuss the nine-year history of Investors 2000 in late 2001, Whitaker and Robinson touted conservative fiscal management, taking the time to invest on your own, and using money and knowledge to help the community and teach kids. It's a more holistic approach to the stock market compared to others. They see Wall Street as an instrument for betterment as well as for financial security. The stock market has also provided a base for building up friendships. Whitaker and Robinson seem closer than ever. They finish each other's sentences and egg each other on as they make a point. At that time, Whitaker was a vice president at Sun Trust Bank. Robinson had recently earned an MBA.

Joining them to talk about stocks and the growth of their investment club were four African American friends from the investment club, aged in their 30s and 40s.

Although he modestly describes himself as a stock-trading novice, Max Williams had already dabbled a bit in the stock market while in college through his cousin, a broker. He started off funneling an extra $50 or $100 here or there into a few stock options. "At the time it was quick money, and for someone who is 19 or 20 years old, quick money is good money." One of the newer members of Investors 2000, he started doing more research on companies once he joined.

Another member of the meeting, a research analyst for a state agency that oversees colleges and universities in Virginia, Jackie Smith-Mason didn't have any interest in the stock market until her 20s, once she finished college and started working. "I can remember watching TV and when something came on about the stock market, it didn't interest me. That was my time to use the remote and change the channel." Being a member of the club has taught her how to get her money to work harder. "There was something out there that I didn't know about, so the investment club helped me to just educate myself about it, and that was really important."

Getting started a bit earlier than most, Byron Rawlinson heard the siren's song of the 1980s stock bubble. After getting out of college, but before he went back to business school, his co-workers urged him to jump into the stock market. They provided pointers and tips, but he waited to make his move. Finally, he bought shares of K-Pro Computers, a high-flying tech stock that soon went the way of Wang computer, down the drain. "I lost my shirt on that one," Rawlinson said. "I did not know what I was doing. I had latched on to a company just based on news, rather than doing any fundamental investigation on the company. The company eventually went bankrupt." He vowed at the time that he would never put money into any specific company, and so he invested in some mutual funds instead over the years. Invited to join Investors 2000, Rawlinson has once again started looking at individual stocks. "I've learned some. I need to learn a lot more, but I'm satisfied."

Another attendee, an analyst for the Federal Reserve, Janet Lacy became familiar with the stock market through her 401(k) plan. While growing up, she knew only about savings bonds or CDs. Whitaker approached her about Investors 2000. It's been a learning experience since then. "I said, 'Wow. I'm happy to be here,'" she recalled.

In the early days, Investors 2000 began meeting at noon on the first Saturday of each month, with a minimum monthly dues payment of $35. Members of the club attended the National Association of Investors Corporation's lessons on selecting stocks for steady gains over the long term. As they grew more sophisticated, they added software to track payments above the $35 minimum to calculate the size of the overall money portion held by each member. They've passed a new rule that members can put in as much money as they want, providing they don't exceed a 20 percent share of the total pot of about $40,000. After 18 months, members can make their first withdrawal, if need be. Each member is responsible for doing a stock selection presentation and then the team votes on moves in the portfolio.

Their top picks over the years include Intel, Hershey, Aflac, and Wendy's. Except for the number-one chip maker, the group mostly shuns technology, Internet stocks, and IPOs in favor of companies with long track records of five years or more. They made some mistakes along the way with investments in software maker Novell and retailer Heilig-Meyers, both of which they later dumped. They've kept J.C. Penney, despite enduring losses from the retailer. Even with the setbacks, Investors 2000 notched compounded annual returns as high as 70 percent in a year.

In addition to researching stocks on the Internet, the group goes on field trips. Using a bit of bravado, a member of Investors 2000 once visited the offices of J.C. Penney as a shareholder. "By the time she finished, the man with J.C. Penney probably thought we owned 100,000 shares," Robinson recalled. "They were willing to send a representative to one of our meetings. She also went to DuPont, since we own stock in the company. She made them give her a tour of the facility."

Investors 2000 prefers to buy stock directly from the company in order to save money on commissions and fees. Disney and Wal-Mart have direct-purchase programs, for example. Whitaker said some 1,100 companies have direct-purchase programs as a way to tap directly into the collective power of Main Street stock market mavens.

In 1998, Investors 2000 won a $1,000 cash prize and was named the Investment Club of the Year by the Coalition of Black Investors. "Ideally, we're all investing for long-term goals," Robinson said. "For me, it may be retirement; for someone else, it may be their child's education, or a down payment for a new home, or an emergency in the household. And we do allow you to take money out of the club if such a situation arises. It's your own money. You can't use it as a savings account; it's more like your own mutual fund."

As a result of knowledge gleaned from the club, many of the 12 members of Investors 2000 now keep their own portfolios.

Investors 2000, which added a word to become Investors 2000 Plus in the new millennium, has seen little reason to stray from the strategy that gave members their first big gain. Eyeing the fundamentals, management style, and market share of Intel, they decided to buy the stock in 1995 despite some negative news about a delay in chip production that weighed on the stock at the time. Down the line, the shares rose handsomely. Since they've held on to their stock for so long, the overall portfolio is still well ahead of their initial investments even after prices eroded in the face of a bear market. The group said they kept ahead of the S&P 500 and the Dow in 2001, not an easy task for ordinary folks or professional money managers.

As of late 2001, these stock pickers were watching their stocks a bit more closely because of all the bad news out there, but instead of selling, they tended to buy more. They added shares of Aflac, for example. "A lot of times when we talk to different people they're a little disappointed when we tell them that, 'No, we're not anxious right now. No, we haven't made any drastic changes to our portfolio. No, we're not going to jump out of a building,'" Whitaker said.

They admit it's difficult to dump stocks at times. "It's hard to let go of a dog, because your emotions are tied to it," Whitaker said. "At that point, you have to go back to the numbers—what were our expectations for this stock, when did we say we'd get rid of it, how much of a loss are we willing to take, has anything changed with management to make this thing bounce back? And then make a sound business decision without emotions. And that's hard."

The group keeps an eye on ratings by Wall Street analysts, but tend to go their own way. "There are a lot of good guys out there and there are a lot of bad guys," Robinson said. "There are a lot of people who are paid big money to keep you confused. That's the truth. That's why many people are frightened of the stock market. You turn the TV on and you're just flooded with information. And they talk in terminology you don't know. It's like, 'Whew, that's too much for me,' and a lot of people just sit on the sidelines."

Bringing their kids with them to their meetings, a collective light went on over the heads of Investors 2000 members when the youngsters started chiming in with their own opinions and questions about Wall Street. The group decided to pool their energy to hold classes for their Second Generation Program. They coach their kids, as well as other young people from their neighborhoods, schools, and churches, in the basics of investment and finance.

"As African Americans in recent history, there have been certain milestones, like basic civil rights during the '60s," Whitaker said. "My dad pushed the importance of education. My dad was one of the first in our family to go to college. He didn't pass on wealth education to me. With us, we have a new awareness, and the big fight now is to make sure that we pass on wealth and how to accumulate wealth. That's the responsibility of this generation."

Robinson added that they want to avoid the same misconceptions and misunderstandings they had about the stock market. "Back in my grandfather's day, [African Americans] were kept out of certain arenas. That's just a fact. And that's not the case anymore. The information is there. We just have to go get it. So realizing that, we decided to set up a program for our children. Even if they don't get to the level of investing, we'd teach them the basics."

Kids are taught about the banking system, how to budget a checking account, and the dangers of overspending and credit cards. Smith-Mason brought in a cash register with play money and food. The kids learned how to stretch their dollars by trying to purchase as much as they could with what they had.

"Children are getting younger and younger as far as having credit cards because we're becoming a more affluent society," Rawlinson said. "And we're giving those things to our children and we're not, as a whole, teaching them to be responsible with those things." His 14-year-old daughter Brittany owns stocks and researches them on the web. His 11-year-old son David is starting to learn about being an entrepreneur and how to make money. "When he is introduced into the working world, he will know how to invest his money properly."

David Rawlinson and Natasha Holloway, daughter of member Barbara Holloway, were winners in an essay contest held by the Coalition of Black Investors. They read their compositions at a function in Washington, D.C., attended by Roger W. Ferguson Jr., vice chairman of the Board of Governors of the Federal Reserve, and New York State Comptroller H. Carl McCall, as well as about 500 other dignitaries and family members. A seventh grader at the time at Richmond Middle School, Natasha read with authority the conclusion of her essay:

"When you invest early, your goal of going to college can be met, without a lot of financial burdens. Lots of times kids only think about today, not tomorrow, or what outfits and shoes they want. If they took some of their allowance and invested in some shoes and clothing companies, they could own part of that company. When I first started to get money all I wanted to do was spend it on toys and CDs, but when my mom told me about investing, I decided to save money and invest in the stocks that I was spending my money on. It was a very good decision. I have learned from the experience that the key to reaching your goals is met by saving and investing in your future."

Besides teaching kids, Robinson and Whitaker offer workshops on the power of investing. "Afterwards, people come up to us and say, 'I just can't believe it's this easy. I can't believe the concept of investing, the way the market works, how to invest, is this simple,'" Whitaker said.

Robinson chimed in, "People give their brokers dollars. You just blindly give them money. I did a workshop, and this guy said, 'I'm not challenging you, but why do I need to know this if there's someone else who already knows this? Why do I have to invent the wheel again?' I said you may not need to know as much detail, but at least know what the company does. Some people don't know where their money is going ...."

Investors 2000 Plus is one of many African American groups touting Wall Street as a route to empowerment. The Coalition of Black Investors (COBI), based in Winston-Salem, North Carolina, was founded in 1997 by investment advisor Duane Davis "to improve financial literacy and foster communication among African American investors." The network of some 7,000 members promotes participation in 401(k)s and putting money away for college tuition. "At least 10 percent of your income should go toward investments," said an article on the COBI website. "If you start at a reasonably early age, and save 10 percent in the proper mix of investments, you will retire in a great financial position." The group also points out challenges in terms of the control of the total economic pie in the U.S.:

> African Americans are 14 percent of the population and only earn 7 percent of the total income in America. We own less than 3 percent of the wealth in America.
>
> —From *Black Labor White Wealth* by Dr. Claud Anderson, Ed., PowerNomics Corp., 1994

In the private sector, New York-based *Black Enterprise* magazine is the publication of choice for Investors 2000 Plus and others. Launched in 1970, the magazine is a cornerstone of a personal-finance empire headed by Earl G. Graves Sr. One of the company's many sub-brands is the Black Enterprise/Greenwich Street Corporate Growth Fund. The $91 million private equity fund founded in 1997 is sponsored by Graves and Citigroup to finance the growth of minority-owned or minority-managed companies with at least $10 million in annual revenue. Not long after the fund was launched, Graves's book, *How to Succeed in Business Without Being White*, published by HarperCollins in 1998, hit the bestseller list.

EAST FLATBUSH CHURCH OF GOD AND THE SU-SU

Such activity in the African American investment world didn't go unnoticed by Patrick Fagan. One of the younger adult members of the Pentecostal East Flatbush Church of God in Brooklyn, New York, Fagan, 28, and friend Wayne Edwards tapped into a familiar practice in their neighborhood and extended it to the stock market.

"It's a long-established custom in the Caribbean community to enter into a group called a su-su (pronounced *soo-soo*) when one wants to save money for some future, usually short-term, purpose. To put it simply, a su-su describes a group of individuals, bound solely by trust, who get together and agree to contribute a certain fixed amount, say $100 each, to a cash pool at an agreed-upon interval. With each contribution, one member of the group gets a turn in the box, and so the cycle continues until each member has his turn."

Fagan, who in late 2001 was a senior policy analyst with the New York City Mayor's Office of Health and Human Services, helped gather 11 church members in August 2000 to launch the group. Casting about for a name, they turned to familiar religious themes. They drew fiscal inspiration from the Old Testament Book of Joshua, Chapter 1, Verse 8, in which the minister of Moses takes up the mantle of leadership from the prophet after his death: "This book of the law shall not depart out of thy mouth; but thou shalt meditate therein day and night, that thou mayest observe to do according to all that is written therein: for then thou shalt make thy way prosperous, and then thou shalt have good success."

Thus was born the Good Success Investment Club, which invests in America Online, American Express, Charter Communications, Dell Computer, Keyspan Corporation, Microsoft, and Oracle. "We want to believe we could be good stewards for the word of God. Our parents and grandparents had been raised with the su-su mentality where they worked hard and tirelessly over the years, and put their monies together for their future. We wanted to take these monies and make them work for us," Fagan said.

One pitfall the group hit early on was analyst ratings. Encouraged by a "strong buy" rating for Ashford.com, the Good Success Investment Club snatched up shares in the Internet retailer. "We invested quite a bit of money in that,"

Fagan recalled. "It went from $24 down to below $1. Why didn't they change their rating? The company wasn't making any money. It was generating revenue, but it was still operating at a loss."

After that learning experience, Good Success scoured balance sheets, particularly of companies in the S&P 500. They eyed price-to-earnings ratios and more. "We also like to see the moral background of the companies," Fagan said. "We don't want to invest in companies that support apartheid. We don't want to invest in companies that support child labor."

One of Fagan's favorites as of late 2001 was cable TV firm Charter Communications, which he lauded for its growing sales, revenue, and subscriptions. For a while the group was tracking shares of Avis, which went up on a buyout deal from Cendant. Of course, the analysts didn't come out with "buy" ratings on the stock until the merger was already announced, Fagan noted. After about two years together, Good Success built up a nest egg of nearly $40,000. In 2002, the club plans to start taking money out of their stock market su-su to launch a scholarship program at their church. Joshua would be proud.

MINT INVESTORS AND THE 91-YEAR-OLD GURU

The Mint Investors of Temple Hills, Maryland, cite the role of 91-year-old investment guru Grafton Daniels of Washington, D.C., affectionately known as both the grandfather and the godfather of investment clubs in the Washington area.

Born in 1911 in Rosslyn, Virginia, Daniels graduated from high school in 1928 and attended Howard University and its Divinity School. Working at the U.S. Geological Survey in 1959, he was first bitten by the stock market bug after a friend approached him about selling mutual funds for the

Hamilton Management Corporation. He joined as the second African American mutual fund sales representative in the Washington, D.C., area.

Investing $50 per month in a Hamilton mutual fund, Daniels started to watch his money grow. He earned a broker's license in 1965 and continued working for the financial services sector at Consolidated Financial Services, ITT-Hamilton Financial Services, and Southwest Financial Services, among others. While collecting numerous civic awards and sales citations, Daniels worked overtime to spread the gospel of investing. He helped found dozens of investment clubs in the Washington area, including a couple of kids' groups. He shared his wisdom from lessons such as a five-figure loss on an investment in diamonds while working as district manager for International Diamond Corporation, which went bankrupt. Daniels touts staying fully invested in stocks and targeting equities with growth rates of 15 percent per year.

He also weaves in a fiery message of racial equality through wealth. A Daniels speech reprinted by *Financial Independence* magazine illustrates his passion for investing:

"This dollar bill, this money is Black Power. You don't have Black Power when you don't have enough money. But as long as you've got money, you have the passport and the key to open any door you want and this will ensure your financial future. ... Money is the affirmative action of the future!"

In an interview with *Financial Independence* editor Zelma Patterson, Daniels suggested that African American physicians pool a portion of their earnings to form a pharmaceutical company aimed at finding a cure for sickle cell anemia. "If black doctors formed a corporation to develop this pharmaceutical company, it would be the means for providing a health product that's needed in the marketplace. This company would also provide for economic development by providing employment for black chemists, biologists, and other professional careers."

Earning accolades from the NAIC, *The Wall Street Journal*, *Black Enterprise,* and many other publications, Daniels was a big inspiration for Jan Barrow and the Mint Investors, among many others. "He has taught us everything we need to know about investments," said Barrow, a founder of the club. "When we started we didn't even know what a stock quote was. But if you look at our portfolio right now, we have done quite well."

Founded in 1996, the core group of the Mint Investors consisted of four sisters, two nieces, and one good friend. Usually it's difficult to pull families together to make money, but this family was different, they pointed out. Now they have 18 members aged 30 to 70. They tout an average return of 21 percent, with more than $98,000 invested as of the start of 2001. Education ranges from high school graduates to undergraduate and Master's degrees. Their yearly incomes range from $40,000 to $100,000. Half of the club members are retired from positions in government, including human resources, housing administration, equal opportunity employment, and budget and finance. The working members serve in positions such as secretary, administrative officer, computer programmer, broadcaster, and doctor.

The Mint Investors used tools by the NAIC to screen stock candidates. They focused on companies with at least 10 years of operating results and 15 percent growth per year. AOL Time Warner was always a winner for them. Although shares of the Internet provider got hit hard during the bear market, they fared better than many. Purchased in 1996, it was one of their first stock picks. Their least favorite stocks were Lucent and WorldCom. "The telecom sector is oversold and too competitive," Barrow noted. "WorldCom needed the Sprint merger. When that did not happen they lost the opportunity of becoming a dominant player in the telecom sector."

After their weekend meetings, the Mint Investors often share a champagne brunch prepared by the hosting member. "This we enjoy. It gives us an opportunity to socialize after education, learning, and decision-making," Barrow said. They have achieved their goal of making money when they started off with their eye on the Federal Mint in Philadelphia, where coins are made. But they've also contributed some of their combined funds to charity. They donated to a family whose mother gave birth to quadruplets to help pay for facilities for the children. They also provided financial support to the junior investment program at St. George Church, and tuition assistance to others.

Some say Wall Street is fueled by greed. Others shrug and say that's the way of the money world. But Wall Street fulfills needs that go beyond dollar signs. For Investors 2000 Plus, Good Success, and the Mint Investors, the stock market built wealth from the ground floor up, in tightly knit groups of folks who share the experience of their communities and the riches of their heritage. At the heart of these clubs' investment efforts is a deep desire to learn the tricky ways of financial markets. The members say they'll never stop learning and never stop acting on their knowledge. It isn't always easy in a financial world ruled by the bottom line, but the recipe for success is out there.

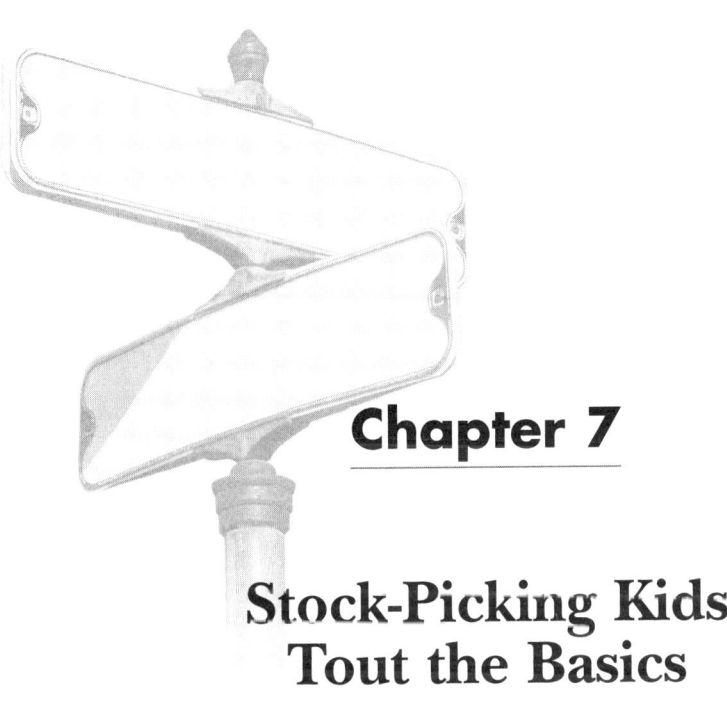

Chapter 7

Stock-Picking Kids Tout the Basics

When asked to raise their hands if they hope to become dot-com millionaires some day, the seventh-graders in Jim Shaughnessy's history class didn't budge. No one dreamed of taking up the once-hot career path that a short time ago captured the fancy of many kids. Internet entrepreneurs were worshipped like rock stars and pro athletes with their flashy cars, big houses, and eight-figure bank accounts by the age of 23—after dropping out of college, no less.

While the dot-com millionaire question would probably get a different response nowadays in Silicon Valley, this was Valley Forge Middle School in Wayne, Pennsylvania. Pharmaceuticals, not silicon, is the big industry in this suburb of Philadelphia, also known for its massive King of Prussia shopping mall. Compared to the slice of California known for computers and technology, this region of green, hilly horse country turned into housing subdivisions more closely typifies the American landscape in the early twenty-first century. For a short time in the 1990s, plenty of kids mused about starting their own websites and becoming rich in the vein of Jerry Yang from Yahoo and countless others. But this was after the bubble, and these kids were interviewed shortly before their holiday break at the end of 2001. And these young people, while consumed with the normal preoccupations of preteen life, were no dummies.

If Yahoo! or Amazon was still going for $200 a share and dot-com companies kept filling the financial headlines with stock prices that shot up faster than a kid on a growth spurt, a few hands in Mr. Shaughnessy's class would have been raised. These kids' heads are filled with classes, homework, friends, families, hobbies, sports, video games, TV, shopping, and on top of all that, screaming headlines on America's war on terrorists. But guess what: They're still surprisingly aware of what's happening on Wall Street. They may not be on some fast track to drum up venture capital to burn, but the kids are all right. They already know a thing or two about survival, and heading up a website sure isn't the way to go about it. If any of them do become entrepreneurs, it's nearly certain their future businesses will use the Internet in some way, shape, or form. Here's the difference from just a couple of years ago: The web is no longer seen as an end unto itself.

Sure, all of the 800 kids at Valley Forge Middle School have access to the Internet, in addition to whatever they may already have at home. Each classroom is equipped with at least one computer; more PCs inhabit the library and labs to bring the total computer population to more than 100. This is probably more than some schools, but not as many as others.

No longer a new, hyped-up thing for kids, the Internet has lost its stigma as a threat to parental authority. It's not a way to revolt, like the way rock or punk rock music was for their moms and dads. The still-young medium has ceased drumming up much hysteria from parents or kids. It's just a tool for chatting with friends through instant messaging, research, e-mail, and keeping up with the news. Maybe they download a tune or two on a music-swapping website modeled after the once-free Napster service. Like other private and public institutions, Valley Forge Middle School deploys firewall software, which not only blocks any harmful adult material, but goes as far as limiting e-mail access altogether.

While the bear market dampened dot-com exuberance, kids still share a good deal of the passion for Wall Street shown by their moms and pops, who invest through their 401(k)s, online accounts, and bricks and mortar brokerages. Maybe the kids were trying to get noticed; but even so, when asked to rank their interest in the stock market on a scale of 1 to 10, with 10 being very interested, most wrote down a 7 or higher. They keep an eye on business news through the Internet, newspaper, or TV, including an occasional stop at financial channels CNBC or CNNfn.

Most didn't mention any specific stocks on their radar screen, but a couple of the kids wore clothing emblazoned with brand markings of retailer Abercrombie & Fitch. "I like Abercrombie & Fitch because I really like their clothes," blurted out Stephanie Norcini, 12. Marty Broser, 13, listed Coca-Cola on his questionnaire, "because I love that soda"; Best Buy, "because I love their electronics"; and Disney, "because I like some of their movies." Eric Merron, 12, rated his interest in the stock market a 9 on his survey form. He noted three family-owned stocks that he tracks—Disncy, GE, and Pepsi—"because they are three big companies that do very well." Kristen McGranaghan, 13, liked GE, because it's "a large company that is successful"; as well as Dell, because they "have good computers"; and America Online, because "I like going on the Internet."

Asked if they'd put a hypothetical $100,000 into the stock market if the money fell into their laps, all said yes for all or some of the money. Jenny Shaab, 12, said she'd put it in a college fund. John Craig Weber, 13, targeted half the money for the stock market. Caitlin Baldwin, 13, said, "I would put one eighth of it in the stock market, but not a lot. I would put three quarters of it in the bank for college and a car. The other one eighth of it I would keep and go to the mall!" (This young lady has obviously been studying her fractions.) Lauren Obee, 12, said she'd "do a little in the stock market, a little for college, and a little for clothes." Michelle Mercogliano, 12, touted the market while displaying a knowledge of its risks. She said she'd invest part of the $100,000 in order "to make more money, even though I have a chance to lose it."

Eric Merron, Michelle Mercogliano, and Kristen McGranaghan all said they'd consider a career as a broker, lawyer, banker, or trader on Wall Street. "I'm fascinated in how it works so it would be a good job for me," said Merron. The lad has already visited the New York Stock Exchange. "It's extremely interesting and important to know about, especially as a grownup," he explained. McGranaghan plans to visit Wall Street "because I would like to experience the craziness of the NYSE."

Asked why they think the stock market bounced back after the September 11 terrorist attacks, Merron replied, "because the confidence of the public came back quickly to go buy and support the stock market after the fear and violence went away." McGranaghan cited rate cuts by the Fed's Alan Greenspan as a boost to the market. Caitlin Baldwin said, "We were shocked at first and were busy with what happened on 9/11/01. Now we are trying to get along with our lives and buying stock because it is pretty cheap." Mercogliano said, "The drop was not based on the economy, but on fear. Once fear passed, people felt the economy would improve."

Several kids said they were looking forward to Mr. Shaughnessy's stock market lessons in the spring, when the teacher heads up the annual effort by Valley Forge Middle School in the Stock Market Game, a 10-week national competition with regional rankings. Kids start out with a $100,000 virtual portfolio and try to build it up by purchasing stocks. The kids whose stocks show the biggest gains win recognition and trips to big cities.

The Securities Industry Association, an umbrella group for Wall Street businesses, founded the 21-year-old program, run by its Foundation for Economic Education. Some six million students nationwide and in 15 other countries have taken part in the competition over the years, including about 700,000 during the 1999–2000 school year. The competition, conducted in both the fall and spring, aims to counteract some of the personal finance sloppiness that persists in America, a land of rampant credit card bills spawned from a penchant for instant material gratification. Even with popularity in investing near an all-time high in the U.S., a survey by Dean Lewis Mandell of the University at Buffalo's School of Management indicated eroding levels of knowledge between 1997 and 2000 about personal finance basics in a poll of some 700 twelfth-graders. Awareness scores on income, money management, saving, investing, spending, and credit issues declined. But a press release by the Stock Market Game glibly points out a much higher financial aptitude among kids who took part in the competition. The SMG kids even performed better than students who had completed entire courses in money management or economics.

Branching out into other avenues, the Stock Market Game is launching an economics program revolving around kids solving mysteries on a website. Morgan Stanley Dean Witter funded the new program with a grant. Pro basketball player Kurt Thomas is a booster of the program as well. The N.Y. Knicks forward, who is an avid investor, lent his name to the Kurt Thomas Investment Challenge at New York's Edward A. Reynolds West Side High School in Harlem. Five winners who took part in the Stock Market Game at the school got paid internships at Merrill Lynch. "I wish I had known about the market when I was young," Thomas told *The Wall Street Journal.* "I just want to show kids they can be accountable for their own money and their own well-being at a young age."

The Stock Market Game is conducted mostly on the Internet nowadays, but when Jim Shaughnessy started taking part with his kids 17 years ago, it was all done on paper and mailed in to game administrators. A teacher since 1970, Shaughnessy, 54, has maintained a youthful demeanor by wearing a collection of bright-colored ties, including a green one with moneybags and another with Dr. Seuss characters. Back in 1985, he turned to the Stock Market Game to boost his efforts as a teacher of gifted and talented kids. "It was a good time to begin investing," he recalled. "I had to learn just to be ahead of the kids." With a bit of beginner's luck, as well as intuition and smarts, Shaughnessy's first team went on to win the number-one ranking in the state that year. No other team from the school has reached such a lofty position since then.

Overall, kids' stock picks tend to be fairly conservative with a preference for food, clothing, and retailing companies that they already know about. "They pick good, quality stocks and hold them," Shaughnessy said. He teaches them how to read annual reports, including writing to companies to request them, and shows them some financial websites to use. One of his better teams in the '90s grew $100,000 into $230,000 in 10 weeks. They wrapped up the season ranked eighth in the state.

Flush with success after his first year leading the Valley Forge team to the top of the state rankings, Shaughnessy decided to play the stock market in real life with a few friends, many of whom were also teachers. Thus was born the Brookwood Investment Association, made up of 15 men who first met at a member's house on Brookwood Drive in Phoenixville back in 1986. Debating on their stock portfolio over bottles of Pennsylvania's Yuengling beer, General Electric has been a consistent pick. The industrial giant has comprised the biggest piece of their portfolio over the years. Merck, Sysco, Walgreen, and Colgate make up their core holdings. They've also owned big chunks of Intel, Automatic Data Processing, Cisco, Johnson & Johnson, and Nokia. Lesser holdings include Brinkler International, Dell, Ford, Qualcomm, and Microsoft.

The investment club took a bath on toy maker World of Wonder, which lured them with its laser tag products. Instead of taking off, the stock price got zapped when the fad fizzled without breaking out of its niche into the mainstream. They also lost big on Hechinger, a home product store that got pushed out the market by Home Depot. "We didn't do our homework on these two, but they made for some great stories," Shaughnessy recalled. By 2001, the group had amassed about $130,000 with an average return over the previous five years of about 25 percent per year. That's a good learning curve. Shaughnessy also bought stocks on his own over the years. Students tipped him off on some of the picks, like Ampex, the maker of data storage tape. He made money on it.

Shaughnessy plugs stocks as a great educational tool. "They're a more exciting mode for teaching because the kids are seeing an instant return. It's either up or down. It's immediately gratifying. It also helps to teach them about personal finance." He weaves anecdotes about stocks into his history lessons. Early colonies in the U.S. at Jamestown, Virginia, and Plymouth, Massachusetts, were the result of joint stock financing with European investors. The Pilgrims ended up in Massachusetts because they ran out of money before they could reach Virginia. Wall Street used to be an actual wall built by the Dutch to protect New Amsterdam from anyone interfering with their commerce, and stocks had been trading in the U.S. since the 1700s. One of the great touchstones of the nation's embryonic years is located across the street from Shaughnessy's middle school at Valley Forge National Park, the scene of a hard winter during the latter part of the Revolutionary War. George Washington, who led the effort, didn't own any equities, as far as Shaughnessy could tell. "He had a lot of land, but no stock," he explained.

Shaughnessy's use of the stock market as a tool to teach kids is by no means unique. In Las Vegas at Brinley Middle School—home of the championship Bruins—Kimberly Hardgrove teaches sixth-grade math and eighth-grade algebra honors. At one point, the school was reluctant to let her conduct after-class stock market sessions. "The new principal said the stock market didn't meet the benchmarks of mathematics," recalled Hardgrove, herself an investor. Hardgrove kept at it and eventually persuaded her superiors that kids wanted to learn about investing in stocks and that mathematics was the key. "They research the stocks, then fill out sheets with profit and losses and we go from there ... after the first week they see how much they have lost or gained; sometimes the five top members will get a pizza party or a *Star Trek* model ship." Hardgrove recalled stories of how her granddad lost millions in the stock market during the Great Depression. Her grandmom, a Harvard University graduate, "made it all back," Hardgrove, in her mid 40s, said. "We used to read the stock pages all day long."

Back in Pennsylvania, Shaughnessy's lessons extend beyond kids to their teachers. Under the Public School

Employees Retirement System (PSERS) of Pennsylvania, teachers have the option of investing through a 403(b) program. Shaughnessy organizes workshops with faculty to point out these and other investing benefits. After 40 years of teaching, a retiree can qualify for 100 percent of his or her salary. Investing for the future, buying a vacation home, and setting up supplemental income are all reasons Shaughnessy mentions for teachers to get involved in the stock market through the state-sponsored fund. Such programs are a huge force on Wall Street. PSERS, for example, totaled $48 billion as of June 30, 2001, down $5.3 billion from the year before in the face of the bear market. It's the fourteenth largest public pension fund in the nation and the twenty-third largest among public and corporate pension funds.

As of early 2002, here were the stats on the biggest of all public funds, the California Public Employees Retirement System (CalPERS), which manages pension and health benefits for 1.2 million public employees, including school administrators and staff, but not teachers. CalPERS's financial girth weighs in at a belly-busting $147 billion, or about 1 percent of the total value of the U.S. stock market. A big chunk of the money, about $90 billion, is invested in domestic and international equities, mostly in index funds. As big as it is, it wasn't strong enough to resist the bear market. CalPERS lost 7.2 percent of its value for the year ending June 30, 2001, in the fund's first evaporation since 1984. CalPERS then lost its chief investment officer, after he served only 16 months on the job, amid a legal battle over compensation. Insider Mark J.P. Anson, a former portfolio manager at Oppenheimer Funds, was promoted to the job to lead the fund in 2002.

CalPERS's fingerprints are all over the market. Like many others on Wall Street, CalPERS turned to real estate investment trusts (REITs) in an attempt to cash in on one of the few sectors to hold its value. CalPERS is so big that it doesn't just buy stock, it buys companies. One recent move included a joint venture to take private a REIT, CalWest Industrial Property, at $24 per share, or $2.1 billion. CalPERS also invests in initial public offerings, such as Wright Medical, an Arlington, Tennessee-based maker of orthopedic devices that raised $94 million in its stock market debut in 2001. The IPO wasn't one of the top gainers of the year, but it turned in a solid performance by rising over its $12.50 offering price. It's one investment by CalPERS that paid off nicely. CalPERS has also been eyeing hedge funds, which often prosper in a down market because, unlike most mutual funds, they short stocks and benefit when prices go down. CalPERS is considering an investment of as much as $5 billion into hedge funds in coming years.

WHEN STUDENTS LEARN *TOO* WELL

Valley Forge Middle School students, the teachers and administrators hired to educate them, the teacher's pension fund, and Wall Street all inhabit an ecosystem of finance that comprises a vast amount of money in the stock market. Occasionally, something can happen that challenges the other organisms living in the system. That something was teenager Jonathan Lebed, the student from hell as far as the Securities and Exchange Commission in the late 1990s under Chairman Arthur Levitt was concerned. At age 15, Lebed was the youngest person ever to be accused of securities fraud.

Lebed grew up in Cedar Grove, New Jersey, and went to school in the area. He started eyeing the stock market after getting an America Online account at age 11. It was also the first stock he bought, as detailed in Michael Lewis's book, *Next: The Future Just Happened* (Norton, W.W. & Company, Inc., 2001). Lebed and two friends formed an investment team called the Triple Threat, a name that echoes professional wrestling, which the boys love. In 1998, they grew a virtual $10,000 into $240,000 and placed in the top 10 among some 3,500 teams in a national student contest on CNBC. Noticing his talent, Lebed's parents opened up an online stock account for their son. Setting up a website called Stock-dogs.com, Lebed posted commentary on penny stocks he came across from e-mails, message boards, and news sites. He started off investing several thousand dollars from a savings bond.

The SEC first contacted Lebed when he was 14, when they came up with his name during a criminal investigation of an adult who had corresponded with the teen about a stock called Havana Republic. Shaken by the encounter, his mom, Connie Lebed, closed his Ameritrade account, but his dad, Greg Lebed, decided the kid had done nothing wrong, so he opened an E-Trade account for Jonathan. The way Jonathan Lebed saw it, he was doing the same thing as any advertisement. As long as you're not lying about the size of a piece of furniture you're selling, or the color of a car, it's not a crime to tell people that the product is great and you should buy it. Lebed figured the same rule should apply to stocks. The SEC disagreed. Touting a stock you own to drive up the price, and then selling it when the price goes up, is known as a pump-and-dump scheme, the SEC said. That's exactly what they accused Lebed of doing.

By this time, Lebed had earned some $800,000 after seeing shares rise by posting messages. He would note an equity is "the most undervalued stock" in history. He touted another as "the next stock to gain 2,000 percent." He invested in Firetector at $2.45 per share, then filled message boards with predictions that the stock would be at $20 "very soon." When the price went up, he cashed out and made a quick $19,000, the SEC charged. At times, he would place a sell limit order on the day he bought the equities to guarantee that he wouldn't miss the price increase while he was in school the next day. In an interview with CBS's *60 Minutes*, Greg Lebed said that at least his son "didn't sit behind a garage smoking pot, or stealing wheels off a car." The family bought a new $40,000 Mercedes, thanks to Jonathan.

Lebed ended up turning over $285,000 to the government in September 2000 to settle civil charges that he had committed fraud. As part of the deal he did not have to admit or deny he had done anything wrong. SEC Chairman Levitt told *60 Minutes* that Lebed "used fictitious names. He made predictions ... without any foundation. The purpose ... was not to help investors ... but rather to line his own pockets as soon as he hyped the price of the stock."

Lebed's lawyer, Kevin Marino, said, "I don't think ... you could draw a principled distinction between what he did and what is done every single day of the week on Wall Street." It could be said that Lebed plugged stocks with little worth; so do Wall Street analysts, some say. He cashed in when the stocks went up, the SEC charged. But others point out that analysts and their employers gain when they win lucrative investment banking contracts from companies they tout.

If the case had gone to court, it's likely that Lebed's lawyer would have attempted to point out such conflicts, thereby putting the prosecution and the entire securities industry on trial in the process. If Lebed had won, it would have challenged some of the very foundations of Wall Street. The SEC avoided this by settling. Perhaps they really didn't have a case at all. Penny stocks are notoriously volatile. Anyone who buys them should know better. Lebed profited on the bubble hysteria of the stock market at the time, but he wasn't the only one doing it. On the other hand, the SEC was attempting to keep the market in tiny companies a little less speculative. You can't blame the agency for trying to carry out its mission to make the stock market a safer place for people's money, but the agency couldn't fully demonize the plucky teen without admitting the inequities of the entire system. Lebed did have to pay $285,000, so technically he was the loser, although he kept quite a bundle.

Internet-trading legends have faded in the face of the bear market. Back at Valley Forge Middle School, students have learned firsthand that it's not as easy to make money as it was for Jonathan Lebed. When I talked to them in December of 2001, eighth-graders Kevin Waegerle, Megan Connors, Scott Deakins, and Mia Della Polla were still nursing losses after taking part in Shaughnessy's stock-picking courses and competition in the annual Stock Market Game the previous spring. They're reluctant to cough up details about their stock picks, but they mentioned Sun Oil. The stock rose amid an upswing in oil prices in early 2001. Waegerle and Connors are both steeped in stocks to some extent because they have relatives who work in the financial services arena. But for the most part, money and investing are relatively low on their priority list. "You don't really talk about stocks, because it's boring," Connors explained. Nevertheless, she thought enough of Krispy Kreme doughnuts to tell her dad to buy some of the stock for her after she saw coverage of the company's initial public offering on television. The image of the company handing out free doughnuts in Times Square to celebrate its stock debut stuck with her, and she tried some of them herself at a kiosk in Philadelphia's 33rd Street Station. "I love their doughnuts," she explained. The stock has been a moneymaker for her family.

Waegerle said his grandmother gave him some AT&T stock. His dad keeps track of it, and he checks up on it occasionally. Deakins, whose uncle works on Wall Street, has visited the New York Stock Exchange. "It didn't really strike my interest until we got there," said Deakins, who caught some of the energy even though he stopped by on a Saturday. An avid golfer, Deakins said he watches shares of Callaway Golf, which have been hard hit. He's already thinking about college and setting aside money for tuition. "My dad owns his own business. He works with computers. So I kind of think I wanna do that. There are a lot of backup things I could do."

The four students kept their cards fairly close to their vest in terms of sharing wisdom they may have gained about money. They offered a few pearls: Some kids seem to spend indiscriminately, and that's bad. Also, don't put all your money into one stock. Buy low and sell high, and research your stocks before you buy them by checking to see if companies have profitable track records. As for becoming rich off the Internet, "that's not very likely to happen," said Connors. "The Internet is shaky these days. You either do really well or really badly," pointed out Deakins. "EBay does really well right now. They make a lot of money with the stuff they sell. You can just make a website and it can do really badly."

None of these kids have the makings of the next Jonathan Lebed, and that's probably a good thing. They're ending childhood and starting adolescence with some solid fundamentals under their belts. One of those fundamentals is common sense. If more adults remembered the same basic lessons, the U.S. economy and the stock market would probably be better off. Mom, Dad, are you listening?

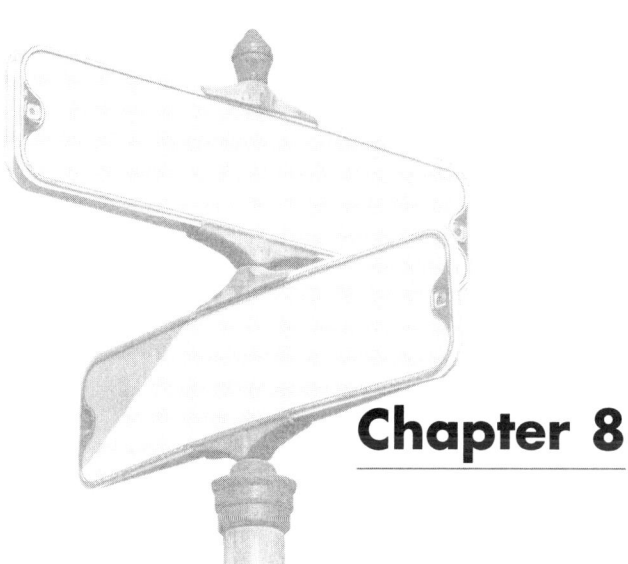

Chapter 8

The Future at Internet Speed, for Better or Worse

Getting stocks to move by posting bulletins on message boards is both a power and a pitfall in the market nowadays. It's a bit like a gigantic game of Telephone, that amusing pastime played in grammar school. A session starts with the leader whispering a tongue-twister message into the ear of the first person: "Freddie fakes it at foosball." The phrase gets passed around the room, ear-to-ear. The punch line comes when the last person repeats out loud what he or she has heard. In most cases, the end result is totally different than the original message; "Freddie fakes it at foosball" may have become "Freddie farts when he flips his football."

Now take that game of Telephone and magnify it by a power of 2 gigahertz, the speed of the fastest personal computer microprocessors. Throw in greed, crazed solo stock pickers, rumor, anger, lost investments, paranoia, and conspiracy theories and you have the vitriolic brew of e-mails and messages that fly through cyberspace at the speed of caffeinated thought. The speed of the Internet's global distribution, combined with the reflexive power of mom and pop investors, armed with instantaneous e-mail and online trading accounts, can be devastating on stock prices.

Cendant, owner of Avis car rental and travel-related businesses that use the Internet to sell airline tickets, saw its NYSE shares decimated to historic lows in 2001 in large part because of individual investors who used the Internet to register their concerns about personal and business travel in the wake of the September 11 terrorist attacks. One day before the attacks, investors on Yahoo! Finance's message boards were saying Cendant's stock deserved a better ride, even in a down economy. One user commented on September 10, 2001, that Cendant is unique in its business because it's a major supplier of discount product as well as a distribution provider.

One day later, after hijacked jets demolished Manhattan's World Trade Center and part of the Pentagon, investors on Internet bulletin boards were harsh about prospects for companies that use the Internet to sell discounted airline and travel services. A Maryland Internet user assessed the terrorist attacks, then told investors who post their sentiments regarding Cendant, "In my opinion for future references, it would be best to avoid purchasing airline tickets, hotel reservations, or car rentals via the Internet. That is the only good way to keep the terrorists out of our great country."

The power of the Internet tends to magnify the swings that stocks take, accelerating both their demise and their recovery, as individual investors flex their ever-more-powerful trading muscles. And that's just when the news is real.

Unfortunately, when retail stock investors turn mean, worse stuff can happen—specifically, fabrications perpetuated by the perils of cyberspace.

Let's start with Houston day trader Fred Moldofsky. He posted bogus news on Lucent earnings on a Yahoo! message board and was ultimately found guilty on securities fraud charges by a jury in federal court. The details were murky during the trial. Moldofsky's lawyer argued that his client simply wanted people to know that Lucent's executives were lying about earnings expectations. He added that his client didn't make any money off the move and never planned to deceive investors. Prosecutors said the fake posting was made to resemble an earnings warning on PR Newswire, a legitimate source of news for media outlets. They added that Moldofsky had traded about 6,000 shares of Lucent stock under pseudonyms before putting the message out, but no trades were made after.

However, no one could argue over what happened in the marketplace at the time of the alleged crime in March 2000. Lucent shares went up once the story got out that Moldofsky's posting was fake and investors realized Lucent wasn't issuing a profit warning. But sure enough, in the days and weeks that followed, Lucent cut profit forecasts as the tech bubble burst. Months later, the troubled company would also reveal that the SEC was investing its accounting practices. So while Moldofsky may or may not have had criminal intent in his heart, he was on to something about Lucent. The Internet served as his own powerful saber, but he cut himself wielding it.

Mark Simeon Jakob, 23, of El Segundo, California, orchestrated a bogus press release on a fledgling news service called Internet Wire. The move caused a crazy paper loss of $2.5 billion in less than an hour to shares of Emulex back in August 2000. Jakob allegedly did it because the stock was going up, and he had bet on it to go down by shorting it. Facing a paper loss of $97,000, Jakob decided to use his knowledge gained from the job he'd left at Internet Wire about a week earlier. He fabricated a doozie of a press release in e-mail form. One, the company was under investigation by the SEC; two, the company's CEO was resigning; and three, Emulex had revised its latest earnings report to reveal a loss instead of a profit. He e-mailed the release posing as a public relations executive familiar with the workings of Internet Wire, timing the release for late at night, when the news reporting service had only a skeleton crew of two on duty.

The next day, a valid-looking press release from a normally trusted source of company information was posted for all news organizations to see. Dow Jones, Bloomberg, CBS MarketWatch, and CNBC, all of which compete by putting out news as quickly as possible, picked up the story. Emulex makes networking and fiberoptic technology, the very stuff that makes up the Internet. And it was cyberspace that did it in that day. Emulex's stock price plummeted to $43 per share, less than half its previous close of $110, in less than one hour, before anyone at the company could say anything to stop it.

Only in the world of online trading and Internet news distribution could such a dramatic swing take place. The Nasdaq halted trading on Emulex for the market to take a breath. But then Jakob's plot died by the Internet, just as it had lived by it. Once the real story got out, the stock quickly climbed back up to $105 per share by the end of a hellish trading day. The FBI tracked the e-mail sent to Internet Wire to a computer located at El Camino College in Torrance, California, from a free Yahoo! e-mail account opened only minutes before it was sent. A search of the account holder revealed Jakob, a former student at the college. Using its regulatory power, the SEC checked Jakob's Datek account. He had shorted 3,000 shares of Emulex a week before the hoax. He pocketed $55,000 by covering his short when the stock plunged on August 25. Not satisfied, he bought 3,500 shares when the stock was beaten down at $50 on the fake news and made another $187,000 in profit on August 28 after the stock climbed back. By September 1, he faced federal charges in what the SEC termed "one of the most devastating financial hoaxes committed in the Internet age." Within a year, Jakob pleaded guilty to stock fraud charges.

Gary Hoke of Raleigh, North Carolina, also pleaded guilty to federal stock fraud charges and was sentenced to five years probation after posting a fake story about his employer, PairGain, to drive up the stock price. Back in 1999, Hoke posted an e-mail message on Yahoo! under the subject of "Buyout News." A click on the link led readers to a website with a phony Bloomberg News story about an Israeli firm offering $1.4 billion for PairGain, double the stock price of the telecommunications equipment maker. Hoke owned PairGain shares and options, but he backed away from selling them once he carried out his plan. The shares came back down after the hoax was revealed. Hoke paid no fine in the case, but after pleading guilty to two felony counts of securities fraud, he was ordered to pay $93,000 restitution out of his future wages to PairGain shareholders who had fallen for his scheme. The SEC complaint listed one victim, an investor from Santa Ana, California, who bought 1,500 shares during the fiasco.

Not all the postings out there come from villains. Kerry Carmichael of Tempe, Arizona, calls himself an "Internet vigilante," not in the Charles Bronson sense, but more like a skeptic in favor of mom-and-pop investors. He defends his recipe for success on Wall Street through long-term, buy-and-hold stock picking. While other hotshots on the web boast about day trading and shorting stocks, ringing up ungodly gains and doing all the things that hedge funds do, Carmichael says he just doesn't want all the risks and hassles of that life. In a posting on the CBS MarketWatch message board made in early 2001, he touted a more conservative approach under the name of his group, the Laughing Stock Investment Club:

"Investment clubs are about education and learning. Yes, we know that some traders can (and sometimes do) outperform long-term, buy-and-hold strategies. But the folks who can trade profitably, and consistently, never seem to realize that they have a 'gift.' Your average Jane or Joe investor can't perform and execute like that. They lack skills, abilities, time, interest, or devotion. For people like that, a long-term, buy-and-hold strategy is much better.

"And that's where investment clubs enter the picture. Yes, we like good returns like everyone else. But the emphasis is on education, not returns. We try to learn from the mistakes of others, and not make too many ourselves. We learn about sectors or ratios and other measures of fundamental analysis. We deliberately pass on trading, because we try to avoid complicating investment factors such as tax liabilities and trading costs. As a club, we tend to favor risk-adjusted returns over total returns. The winner of the race is not really a winner if he or she cannot sleep at night worried about their investments."

Carmichael knows a thing or two about using the stock market to produce solid, dependable gains. Striking it lucky in 1995, he won a $2.5 million, pre-tax jackpot in the Arizona State Lottery. Managing his money himself, he's been able to retire from his job as a computer programmer and live comfortably without draining his prize. Little else has changed. He stayed in the same house. His wife bought a car. His big splurge was to go to the 1996 Super Bowl to see the Steelers play. (They lost.) Carmichael also turned his attention to starting an investment club with some of his former co-workers at the local community college. The club's holdings include Amgen, Applebee's, Apollo Group, Barnes & Noble, Intel, and Johnson & Johnson. Laughing Stock Investment Club uses software from the National Association of Investors Corporation to evaluate its holdings. The software told them to sell Cisco. They didn't, and learned their lesson. Like countless others, Carmichael checks the message boards and sometime pipes up when he has something good to say.

Some message senders are anonymous, for many reasons. Even if their given name appears to be normal-looking instead of some strange handle like "Shufflefish" or "Aqualcool_2000," the name could still be fictitious. Whatever their true identities, they share true wisdom at times. Rupert_E warned readers on SiliconInvestor.com of the dangers of investing in initial public offerings, shortly before the IPO bubble burst. His cautiousness was ahead of its time when he warned people about hyped-up shares of IPOs that would drop once they reached the open market. The stocks would make money only for insiders who got the shares at their offering price, at the expense of retail investors.

"It's not the red-hot, heavily hyped-up IPOs that we individual investors can make money on, it's the high-quality IPOs that are overlooked or ignored when they come out .... In order to minimize risk, I only really want to buy quality companies. This way if I get stuck with a stock that goes down, at least I know it has the potential to return to higher levels. ... It is important to decide what you're willing to pay for the stock before it starts trading. That way you don't get carried away."

Rupert_E's posting back in February 2000 heralded the more sober-minded approach to IPOs that continues into 2002. Investors spit out shares of flashier IPOs in favor of companies with track records and profits. Brokerages also discouraged flipping of IPOs, in which investors dump shares as soon as they get them for a quick profit.

While anonymous messages often contain good information, they're also used by retail investors to blast any and all things that bother them. But anonymity on the web isn't absolute. Yahoo!, for example, will reveal personal information, "under special circumstances, such as to comply with subpoenas," the Internet portal says in its privacy policy. Fed up with criticism from unnamed sources on messages boards, companies have attempted to fight back. Apple Computer, for example, once filed suits against individuals it accused of revealing trade secrets on message boards.

Privacy advocates argue that websites and Internet service providers seem too willing to reveal identities of users in defamation suits, whether or not the underlying case has merit. One case involved Gregory P. Hackett of Hudson, Ohio, who insulted his employer, web consultant Answer-Think, on the Yahoo! message board. Using the name Aquacool_2000, he labeled AnswerThink as a "poorly managed, under-leveraged company." Other messages accused AnswerThink of missing deadlines and accused a manager at the company of being "an adolescent whose favorite word is 'turd.'" Fed up after dozens of negative messages in a few months, AnswerThink filed a defamation lawsuit in Federal Court against "John Doe" and successfully subpoenaed Yahoo! for the identity of Aquacool_2000. Once they got the name of their critic and saw it was someone who actually worked for them, they fired Hackett. He responded by suing AnswerThink and Yahoo! for violation of privacy.

David Sobel, general counsel of the Electronic Privacy Information Center, said in a press release that the case marked the first time an individual filed suit against Yahoo! for disclosing the identity of a user. Hackett's complaint reminded the court that message boards give anyone the power to protest or rebut a statement. It added that pen names have been used throughout history, from Shakespeare to Mark Twain. The case was settled out of court, and Yahoo! quietly changed its policy on turning over identities. In the past, it would do so immediately after receiving a subpoena requesting someone's real name. Now, Yahoo! notifies the user and gives them 15 days to respond. America Online and Microsoft's MSN portal also have similar policies.

Other cases have followed as anonymous postings continue to draw court actions. In April 2001, a federal judge ruled 2themart. com, trading for pennies a share, did not have the right to force SiliconInvestor.com to unmask "Truthseeker," "Cuemaster," or "Noguano." Their messages included the accusation that 2themart. com "is a Ponzi scam that Charles Ponzi would be proud of." Cuemaster claimed the company was "dumped by their accountants ... these guys are friggin' liars." Another message urged investors to "bail out now."

In his ruling against 2themart.com, Federal Judge Tom Zilly said, "The Internet is a truly democratic forum for communication. It allows for the free exchange of ideas at unprecedented speed and scale. For this reason, the constitutional rights of Internet users, including the First Amendment right to speak anonymously, must be carefully safeguarded. Courts should impose a high threshold on subpoena requests that encroach on this right."

As the bear market took a deeper hold and attention turned toward the recession, layoffs, and surviving terrorist attacks, the furor over message boards has died down. Mike Quigley, a vice president of Infospace, which owns Silicon Investor, said the bulletin board service that charges $10 per month for the privilege of posting messages hasn't seen any other lawsuits lately after the 2themart.com case in the second quarter of 2001. Infospace weighs each request to divulge identities of users on its merits after consulting lawyers. "We want to protect the privacy of subscribers. Underneath that, we reserve the right to access and disclose individuals to comply with the law," he explained. Overall, the mood of the message board has grown more somber compared to the boasting that went on during the heyday of the bull market. "We've seen more focus on fundamentals and cash positions to help people weather the storm," Quigley said. Catering to a narrower audience than free message boards such as Yahoo!, Silicon Investor's core audience tends to be well-educated males with incomes of $75,000 or more. "Our customers spend a lot of time researching. These guys dig up a lot of great information, and they do pay attention. They listen to conference calls. You have people sending headlines on a real-time basis. They wish they were in the trading pits."

As a dismal 2001 came to a close on the CBS MarketWatch message boards, the most popular postings on New Year's Eve were on the topics of religion and philosophy, not stocks. Readers batted theories around about *Harry Potter*, the hit movie of the season. Also big on these boards, at CBS MarketWatch, was Wal-Mart, on people's minds because of the shopping season; and Oracle, which announced a round of layoffs on December 31.

INTERNET SPEED AHEAD

Anyone who's experienced the heat of the market at the New York Stock Exchange, or any other trading room floor, can feel the intensity. People chain-smoke on their breaks (if they have them), rush around, and curse at the speed of light as they keep the wheels of capitalism whirring along. Retail investors, sitting at their computers waiting to make their move, are removed from the action, but they yearn to be part of it. They're at home or in their offices, behind their desks, frustrated at being spectators even as they spend thousands of their own hard-earned money. They can't go out on cigarette breaks from the pits and stand shoulder-to-shoulder with their fellow warriors in the market trenches. But they can do one thing that the professional traders do, and learn to do it well. They can curse. And they can send out their rants in the form of e-mail to anyone who gets in their way. CBS MarketWatch reporters and columnists get a front-seat view of some of the more crazed stock market mavens out there. It's a window into a world of strange comments, allegations, and fresh insights on the stock market, both good and bad.

Julie Rannazzisi, whose Market Snapshot column for CBS MarketWatch tracks every move by the Dow and the Nasdaq, thumbtacks some of her favorite e-mails above her desk in her office on West 57th Street in Manhattan. Some readers accuse her of being bearish, others say she's bullish, or worse yet, a cheerleader. Some seem to think she controls whether stocks rise or fall. "Please make the stock market go back up. Thanks for your help!" wrote one reader. Another reader reacted to Rannazzisi's reports on downswings in the market with a dark forecast. In an e-mail, the reader wrote to Rannazzisi that she has to think like a bear. Spelling "bear" in capital letters for emphasis, the reader called on investors to completely give up on the stock market, saying Rannazzisi should say there is no hope for 2001. Complete with extremely dire predictions for the Nasdaq down to 250— and the Dow down to 1000, its level prior to 1983—the naysayer repeated that the public must completely give up on the stock market because the bear market of 2000–2001 was like the Great Depression. The reader softened these dire predictions by closing "Sorry."

StockWatch columnist and CBS MarketWatch editor-in-chief Thom Calandra collects basketfuls of e-mails from readers who either love or hate the consistent message in his articles that the bear market is far from over and that stock prices are too high after bouncing back from the September 11 terrorist attacks.

Calandra maintains the stock market is vulnerable to a big sell-off in 2002 based on sentiment indicators and other forecasting tools. That made one reader send in an angry e-mail. Titled "Calandra is the anti-Christ," it read in part, "You are an example of the human blight that thwarts progress. You always see darkness, never light." In another e-mail, a person told Calandra, "I think you should shut up if you've nothing positive to say. Maybe you should just move to Japan."

Craig Harris, president of Harris Capital Management, a futures broker and commodity trading advisor, had more positive things to say about a Calandra column that contained the adage, "As someone once said, and it might have been Yogi Berra or Warren Buffett, 'The first rule is not to lose, and the second is not to forget the first rule.'"

"It's nice to read something that makes sense," Harris wrote in an e-mail. "I've been telling my clients to be careful with this market. I don't want to be short on the market, however, because since the 11th, I have seen many signs that this market is sponsored by the Fed and the G-7 (the seven leading industrial nations) both directly and indirectly. They simply can't afford to let the bubble pop. So now we're building a bigger bubble from lower levels ... the outcome of which is scary."

Speaking on the *CBS MarketWatch Weekend* TV show in late 2001, Calandra said he thought Cisco was overvalued at about $18 per share. One reader, who said he's been a retail broker on Wall Street for the past four years, called the position laughable. "How can you say Cisco is overvalued? Are you kidding? The company is a cash cow with billions in cash, zero long-term debt, and No. 1 in their business. They are also the No. 1 positioned company to take advantage of the Internet when it blossoms in Asia. At $18 per share it IS cheap. This was an $80 stock and will be again." The reader ended his missive with a popular quote from Warren Buffett: "This is the time to get rich."

Not everybody disagreed with Calandra. David R. wrote, "I have been telling fellow traders that this (fourth quarter 2001) rally is a bear trap. I keep saying the market can't sustain these lofty levels. However, the market and the myriad of so-called market experts continue to prove me wrong. I am currently shorting the QQQ (Nasdaq) because I look for us to re-test the post-attack lows …. Stick to your guns. You're the voice of reason and will be proven right."

Mike P. told Calandra, "I enjoyed your article on interest rate spreads and what they might portend for the market. It would have even been more worthwhile if the historical references to relative valuations referenced more than P/E ratios. What were interest rates and inflation rates like in 1941 and 1974? Wouldn't they impact how much investors might be willing to pay for stocks and the perceived value of return on their investment over time?"

Lastly, someone writing under an e-mail pseudonym took this shot at Calandra: "You are nothing more than a financial word terrorist. It's writers like you that make me wish the government controlled the press. Take a vacation … how about Iraq!"

What a nice guy.

It's maddening trying to figure out who is wrong or right about the stock market. The Dow and Nasdaq tend to do whatever they're going to do, and the experts can only explain what's going on *after* it happens. Through it all, the one consistent recipe for success touted by individual investors continues to be common sense. Don't get too carried away. Don't bet the farm. Try to play well with others, and don't get too greedy. As mom-and-pop stock pickers continue to flex their muscles, they're learning to walk with more confidence. They're finding their footing through their favorite websites, or by forming their own kitchen table mutual funds with stock compadres in their families or investment clubs. They're taking their best shots by finding quality companies and holding on to them. They're learning to let go of underperformers.

The stock market will take whatever you throw at it. You can nibble around the edges, or plunge your entire heart, soul, and wallet into it. Someday you will die, but the market will live on. Despite all the doom, gloom, and uncertainty in the early twenty-first century, the more level-headed folks remember that the stock market has always managed to come back, and it will again. Consumer confidence is rising quickly as the United States continues its war against terrorism. Hope for a recovery is building.

At the very best, the bull market will return in a more subdued form than the raucous '90s as the intoxication of online trading, Internet access, instant information, deep online research, and analyst recommendations wears off in the bear market hangover. Hopefully, these tools, in the hands of a more responsible, market-savvy public, will help equalize the playing field as part of a truly free marketplace with a democracy of information. More likely, the pace of the market will continue to build, stoked by the power of the Internet to get people worked up. We're optimistic that the next market bubble won't be as big as the one that pumped foul air into thousands of stocks in 1999 and 2000.

As most Americans brace for a bear market, one that could last years, the financial worth of stocks remains a constant force. Dumpster diving for value companies, rather than a focus on growth stocks, is the new name of the game. Mid-cap and small-cap stocks have provided some cause for optimism. Flashy technology companies are still suspect. Stock gems are waiting to be discovered in the trash bin of the market.

Ordinary folks—retail investors who have been shopping for stocks based on low prices relative to projected earnings growth—are in control now. These are the same investors who were laughed at in the late 1990s for being too conservative. The trick is to find the value beneath the grime. You can't just get a stock because it's cheap. The company has to have promise. It may take a few quarters before the price recovers, but if you've found the value before others, you'll see gains. It's not easy, but what is?

It may be that the best most of us can do is heed the words of market historian Robert Rhea, who wrote the 1932 stock market classic *The Dow Theory:* "No profession requires more hard work, intelligence, patience, and mental discipline than successful speculation."

Hey, what a nice guy. Now let's go out and make a fortune, before we lose our shirts.

Index

A

AAII (American Association of Individual Investors), 15
African American investors, 77-91
American Association of Individual Investors (AAII). *See* AAII (American Association of Individual Investors)
Anderson, Claud, 86
Anderson, Georgia, 38, 43
Andrew Jackson Investment Club, 33
Ayers, Cathy, 37

B

Baldwin, Caitlin, 96
Barrow, Jan, 99
Beardstown Ladies investment club, 13-14
Beckham, Henry, 33
Bhonsle, Ranjit, 22
Bjornerud, Anthony, 74-75
Blodget, Henry, 52
Bluewater/Hibbard Railroad Indicator, 3-6
Bogle, John, 51
Buffett, Warren, 16, 51

Busby, Jay, Bluewater/Hibbard Railroad Indicator, 3-6

C

Calandra, Thom, 62, 117-119
Calhoun, Ken, 61, 68
California Public Employees Retirement System (CalPERS). *See* CalPERS
CalPERS (California Public Employees Retirement System), 101
Campbell Cowperthwaite, 46-47, 49, 56
Carmichael, Kerry, 111-112
Chicago Mercantile Exchange, 15
child investors, 93-106
Circle City Investment Club, 26
Coalition of Black Investors. *See* COBI
COBI (Coalition of Black Investors), 84-85
Cohen, Abby Joseph, 51
Common-Sense Investment Guide, Beardstown Ladies investment club, 14
Connors, Megan, 105
Crosland, Mary Belle, 32

D

Daniels, Grafton, 88-91
Davis, Duane, 85
day traders, 59-75
    Calhoun, Ken, 68-69
    Jee, Rupert, 71-72
    Johns, Ray, 69-70
    McCuistion, David, 72-74
    Park, "Tokyo Joe," 61-62, 64-68
    Shadkin, Mikhail, 72
    sideline work, 70-75
DayTradingUniversity.com, 61
Deakins, Scott, 105
dividend-paying stocks
    largest payout ratios, 18
    top companies, 18
Dow Jones Industrial Average, 7
Dow Theory, The, 121
Drayton, William, 30
Duncan, Bobbi, 43

E

Electronic Privacy Information Center, 114
Enron, 10
Excelsior Large Cap Growth fund, 47

F

Fagan, Patrick, 86-88
Ferguson Jr., Roger W., 84
Forest Street Investors, 25
Fouchek Investment Club, 21-23

G

Gambacorta, Anthony, 10
gold stocks, 19

Good Success Investment Club, 87
Graves Sr., Earl G., 86
Greenspan, Alan, 13

H

Hackett, Gregory P., 114
Hardgrove, Kimberly, 100
Harpe, Karen, 37
Harris, Craig, 118
Hill, Chuck, 53
Hirsch, Yale, 58
Hogback Investment Club, 26
Hoke, Gary, 111
holding periods
    stocks, 6
Holloway, Barbara, 84
Holloway, Natasha, 84
How to Succeed in Business Without Being White, 86

I

initial public offerings (IPOs). *See* IPOs (initial public offerings)
Internet
    business trends, 107
    growth of, 9
    message boards, 113
    online trading, 107-121
    online trading accounts, 8-11
    privacy issues, 114
    securities fraud, 109-114
    trading over, 10-11
Internet companies
    investment fad, 20
investment clubs
    AAII (American Association of Individual Investors), 15
    Andrew Jackson Investment Club, 33

Beardstown Ladies investment club, 13-14
Circle City Investment Club, 26
demographics, 14
earnings rates, 15
Forest Street Investors, 25
Foucheck Investment Club, 21-23
Good Success Investment Club, 87
growth of, 14
Hogback Investment Club, 26
Laughing Stock Investment Club, 112
No Cents Investment Club, 16-18
Piggy Bank Investments Club, 30-44
Polaris Investment Club, 24-27
tech stocks, 19-23

J

Jackson, Susan, 32-34, 36-43
Jakob, Mark Simeon, 109-111
Jee, Rupert, 71-72
Johns, Ray, 69-70
Johnson, George Dean, 31, 40

K

Kosoy, Karen, 66
Krispy Kreme, phenomenon of, 40-44

L

Lacy, Janet, 80
Laughing Stock Investment Club, 112
Lebed, Connie, 103

Lebed, Greg, 103
Lebed, Jonathan, 102-105
Letterman, David, 71
Levitt, Arthur, 102
Lewis, Michael, *Next: The Future Just Happened,* 102
Lynch, Peter, 16, 48, 51

M

Mandell, Dean Lewis, 97
Marino, Kevin, 104
MarketWatch.com, 10
May, Tony, 26
McCuistion, David, 72-74
McDaniel, Martha, 38
McGranaghan, Kristen, 95-96
Meeker, Mary, 52
Mercogliano, Michelle, 96
Merron, Eric, 96
message boards (Internet), 113
Milliken, Roger, 31
Moldofsky, Fred, 109
mutual funds
    Excelsior Large Cap Growth fund, 47

N

NAIC (National Association of Investors Corporation), 24
Nasdaq index, 8
National Association of Investors Corporation, 113
National Association of Investors Corporation (NAIC). *See* NAIC (National Association of Investors Corporation)
Next: The Future Just Happened, 102
No Cents Investment Club, 16-18

O

Olejnik, Mary, 33, 35
online stock-trading accounts
  growth of, 9
online trading, 107-121
online trading accounts, 8-11

P–Q

Park, "Tokyo Joe," 61-68
Patterson, Zelma, 89
Piggy Bank Investments Club, 30-44
Polaris Investment Club, 24-27
Polla, Mia Della, 105
Ponzi, Charles, 115
professional stock brokers, 45-58
  terrorist attacks (9/11/01)
    effects on, 54-58
PSERS (Public School Employees Retirement System) of Pennsylvania, 101
Public School Employees Retirement System (PSERS) of Pennsylvania, 101
pump-and-dump scheme
  stocks, 103

R

Rannazzisi, Julie, 117
Rawlinson, Byron, 80
Rawlinson, David, 84
Rhea, Robert, 121
Richardson, Jerry, 31
Robinson, Carolyn, 78-84
Rukeyser, Luis, 46

S

S&P (Standard & Poor's) 500 Index, 8
San Francisco
  Internet companies, 20
Securities and Exchange Commission (SEC) 45, 53-54, 62-63, 66, 68, 102-104
securities fraud, Internet, 109-114
Securities Industry Commission, 97
Shaab, Jenny, 96
Shadkin, Michail, 72
Shaughnessy, Jim, 93-101
  Stock Market Game, 97-100
Sobel, David, 114
Sonders, Liz Ann, 46-49, 56-58
southern United States, stockholders percentages, 29
Spartanburg, South Carolina
  equity owners, 29-31
  origin, 30
Standard & Poor's (S&P) 500 Index. *See* S&P (Standard & Poor's) 500 Index
Stock Market Game
  Shaughnessy, Jim, 97-100
Stock Trader's Almanac, 58
stockholders demographics, 7
stocks
  dividend-paying stocks, 18-19
  gold stocks, 19
  holding periods, 6
  tech stocks, growth of, 19-23
  U.S. ownership statistics, 6

T

tech stocks
  big names, 9
  growth of, 19-23
Teeples, John, 52
terrorist attacks (September 11, 2001), effects of, 54-58
Thomas, John, 30
Thomas, Kurt, 98
Townsend, Brian, 23

U–V

United States, regional stock holders percentages, 29

Vanguard, 48, 51
Vasquez, Kevin, 21

W–X–Y–Z

Waegerle, Kevin, 105
Wall Street Week, 46
Weber, John Craig, 96
Whitaker, Adrienne, 78
Williams, Max, 79

Zilly, Tom, 115